Teaching for Educational Equity

Teaching for Educational Equity

Case Studies for Professional Development and Principal Preparation, Volume 1

Jennifer L. Martin and Jane Beese

ROWMAN & LITTLEFIELD
Lanham • Boulder • New York • London

Published by Rowman & Littlefield
A wholly owned subsidiary of The Rowman & Littlefield Publishing Group, Inc.
4501 Forbes Boulevard, Suite 200, Lanham, Maryland 20706
www.rowman.com

Unit A, Whitacre Mews, 26-34 Stannary Street, London SE11 4AB

British Library Cataloguing in Publication Information Available

Library of Congress Cataloging-in-Publication Data

Names: Beese, Jane, 1965- author. | Martin, Jennifer L. (Professor of education) author.
Title: Teaching for educational equity: case studies for professional development and principal preparation, volume 1 / Jennifer L. Martin and Jane Beese.
Description: Lanham, Maryland : Rowman & Littlefield Education, [2016] | Includes bibliographical references and index.
Identifiers: LCCN 2016011554 (print) | LCCN 2016014757 (ebook) | ISBN 9781475821871 (cloth : alk. paper) | ISBN 9781475821888 (pbk. : alk. paper) | ISBN 9781475821895 (electronic)
Subjects: LCSH: Critical pedagogy--Case studies. | Social justice--Study and teaching--Case studies. | Teachers--In-service training. | School principals--In-service training.
Classification: LCC LC196 .B44 2016 (print) | LCC LC196 (ebook) | DDC 370.11/5--dc23

Printed in the United States of America

Contents

Preface

In early 2014, the Department of Education's Office for Civil Rights released data illustrating how racism and structural inequalities impact schools today. Some of the most startling findings from these data include the following: although African American students account for only 18 percent of U.S. pre-K enrollment, they account for 48 percent of *preschoolers* [our emphasis] with multiple suspensions; African American students are expelled three times more than their white counterparts; African American and Latina/o students account for 40 percent of enrollment at schools offering gifted programs, but only 26 percent of students in said programs.

African American, Latina/o and Native American students attend schools with higher percentages of first-year teachers (3 to 4 percent) than their white counterparts (1 percent); and African American students are more than three times as likely to attend schools where less than 60 percent of teachers meet all state requirements for certification and licensure. The above findings have great implications for our K-12 schools, for higher education, and for society in general (U. S. Department of Education Office for Civil Rights, 2014).

According to Asher (2007) pre-service teachers, most of whom are white, often come into their teacher education programs with little to no exposure to multicultural education or diversity. Perhaps more concerning, some students go through their entire teacher education programs without specific training in multicultural education or culturally responsive pedagogy, thus graduating unprepared for successful teaching of students unlike themselves.

If pre-service teachers are provided the opportunities to "explicitly, and critically interrogate the historical and present-day intersections of race, culture, gender, and foster a self-reflexive engagement with difference" (Asher,

2007, pp. 65-66), teachers can uncover more significant and self-reflexive ways to know the self and others in relation to race, power, and privilege.

Previous research has suggested that not only are disciplinary techniques negatively associated with educational outcomes, but also they are inequitably levied toward students of color (Casella, 2003; Lewis, Butler, Bonner, & Jubert, 2010; McCarthy & Hoge, 1987; Monroe, 2005; Perry & Morris, 2014; Skiba, Michael, Nardo, & Peterson, 2002).

Our goal for this volume is to challenge the status quo and to problematize the attitudes that contribute to disparate treatment of students in our current educational milieu that contribute to the unfair treatment based upon race, gender, sexual orientation, language status, disability, and other identity markers.

It is our hope that this volume will highlight the pressing need for multicultural education and the pressing need to expose all educators to culturally responsive pedagogical practices, particularly in light of the pervasive notion that we live in a post-racial society, despite evidence to the contrary: the June 2015 massacre in Charleston, South Carolina, the exposure of police brutality through the killings of unarmed Black citizens, and the apparent cover-up of the murder of Sandra Bland.

Plucked out of the news, from our own memories, or current lives, the cases contained in this volume represent the lived experiences of real students, teachers, and administrators. We struggle with issues of social justice, as we invite the reader to do, and with how to create and maintain equitable environments for all of our students in all of our schools.

REFERENCES

Asher, N. (2007). Made in the (multicultural) U.S.A.: Unpacking tensions of race, culture, gender, and sexuality in education. *Educational Researcher, 36*(2), 65–73.

Casella, R. (2003, November). Punishing dangerousness through preventive detention: Illustrating the institutional link between school and prison. *New Directions for Youth Development. Special Issue: Deconstructing the School-to-Prison Pipeline* (99), 55–70.

Lewis, C. W., Butler, B. R., Bonner, I. I., Fred, A., & Joubert, M. (2010). African American male discipline patterns and school district responses resulting impact on academic achievement: Implications for urban educators and policy makers. *Journal of African American Males in Education, 1*(1), 7–25.

McCarthy, J. D., & Hoge, D. R. (1987). The social construction of school punishment: Racial disadvantage out of universalistic process. *Social Forces, 65*(4), 1101–1120.

Monroe, C. R. (2005). Why are "bad boys" always black? Causes of disproportionality in school discipline and recommendations for change. *The Clearing House: A Journal of Educational Strategies, Issues and Ideas, 79*(1), 45–50.

Perry, B. L., & Morris, E. W. (2014). Suspending progress collateral consequences of exclusionary punishment in public schools. *American Sociological Review, 79*(6), 1067–1087.

Skiba, R. J., Michael, R. S., Nardo, A. C., & Peterson, R. L. (2002). The color of discipline: Sources of racial and gender disproportionality in school punishment. *The Urban Review, 34*(4), 317–342.

U. S. Department of Education Office for Civil Rights. (2014, March). Date snapshot: School discipline. http://ocrdata.ed.gov/Downloads/CRDC-School-Discipline-Snapshot.pdf

Acknowledgments

That Justice is a blind goddess
Is a thing to which we black are wise:
Her bandage hides two festering sores
That once perhaps were eyes
                                        –Langston Hughes, "Justice"

The history of this text begins with the power of story. As a teacher for more than twenty years, many of the stories contained in this volume are based on my own experiences. Now as a teacher educator, I often wished to find case studies where my students could struggle with issues that they would eventually face within their future classrooms.

Finding few cases that I could use for pedagogical purposes, I was resigned to write my own. However, it was not until I found a writing partner in my friend and colleague Dr. Jane Beese that I found the courage and strength to do so. I thank Dr. Beese for believing in this project and for providing me with guidance and critique. Dr. Beese truly provided the structure for the narrative that was instrumental in making these cases worthy of classroom use.

As professors, we would be doing our students a disservice if we were not connected to the world around us. At this time of this writing, I find myself tremendously troubled by the state of the racial unrest in the United States. It seems that every day there is another incident of police brutality extinguishing the lives of Black bodies in a society that purports to be post-racial. Although the cause of social justice is more than just about race, I dedicate this volume to those who advocate for racial justice in schools and society, for it is clear that we have so much more work to do.

I have many to thank for their support of my work. First, I thank my institution, The University of Mount Union. I thank my students, past and present, for challenging me to do a better job every single day. I thank my friends and my family for understanding my need to do social justice work, despite the repercussions that undoubtedly impact them.

I also thank Dr. Thomas F. Koerner, vice president and publisher of the education division at Rowman & Littlefield Publishing Group, for believing in this project from the beginning.

Finally, I thank the reader. I hope that you gain much from your engagement with this text. We challenge you to do the work. Are you strong enough?

–Jennifer L. Martin

As a student and a teacher, I have found case studies to be an important tool in the classroom. They provide the context for complex problem solving and help guide teachers and administrators in the decision-making process. Case study pedagogy provides a method of application when supported by discourse and reflective practice enhances that students' understanding and intensifies the learning process.

I have been blessed with the support of many. First, I want to thank my institution, Youngstown State University. I thank my colleagues for their constant encouragement and the example they set by the compassion they show toward their students. I also want to thank my three children, Jonathon, Jacob, and Emily, for their understanding of the long hours I have put into writing and for their love. Next, I want to express my gratitude to Jennifer for her talent and dedication to this project.

Through our many writing endeavors, we have challenged and supported each other. Jennifer has made me a more thoughtful practitioner—thank you. Finally, I want to thank Rowman & Littlefield for believing in our vision.

I challenge the reader to consider the vast implications of social injustice and their role in making a difference. Every small act has the capacity to manifest great things. It is every educator's responsibility to make their classroom, school, or district a safe and just place for our children—a place where children are inspired to use their intellect and creativity to reach their fullest potential.

–Jane A. Beese

Introduction

This volume includes cases pertaining to race, class, gender, sexual orientation, discrimination and harassment, culturally responsive pedagogy, intersectionality, et cetera. Each case requires the reader to look beyond the facts, by providing guidance on current research and policy. Each case provides the reader with additional information that will assist them in making informed decisions. Additionally, each case provides facilitators with guiding questions to assist them in their pedagogy and for subsequent class discussion. Although some of these cases are based upon real events, all names have been changed to protect the anonymity of those individuals and institutions.

PEDAGOGICAL USES OF THIS VOLUME

Teachers and school leaders are confronted by various issues pertaining to social justice every day. This volume will help school leaders to handle these issues ethically, and is intended to be used by administrators for the professional development of teachers, teacher leaders, and aspiring principals.

This volume can be also be used in the higher education classroom in order to prepare current and aspiring teachers and administrators to lead for social justice. This volume utilizes the case study approach, which has been found to "sharpen problem-solving skills and to improve the ability to think and reason rigorously" (Harvard Graduate School of Education, 2013).

This volume proposes to enable leaders or professors to assist their teachers or students in examining and grappling with the issues facing teachers and administrators today pertaining to social justice. This volume will challenge the strategies teachers and school leaders employ as they meet head-on both the problems of day-to-day instruction and school leadership and more unexpected situations and issues through the case study approach.

By utilizing the case study approach, this volume will focus on problem solving as an opportunity for future teachers and leaders to focus their efforts on issues that matter through communication, policy formation, organizational systems, attention/reflection to the core work of schools, and on the legal/ethical responsibilities of teachers and administrators. In this way the text seeks to develop teachers' and school leaders' abilities to respond to the issues and opportunities that arise in their daily practice.

Additionally, the volume will draw on the appropriate foundational theory, applicable research, and policy, to underscore why the strategies contribute to effective practice and school improvement. By exploring these complimentary areas of practice, this text seeks to enhance the social justice understanding of teachers and school leaders concerning their problem solving skill set and knowledge base.

Understanding how organizations work and the methods school leaders might effectively use to address problems pertaining to social justice in their school organization is central to professional development. In no case is this more evident that in the problem solving context.

This volume rests on the assumption that the heart of teaching and leading lies in the decisions one makes daily and strategically in relation to the problems the organizational context presents. In an effort to define the niche for this proposed volume two sets of related literature have been identified: 1) the broader organizational theory literature; and 2) the more focused social justice literature.

It is envisioned that this volume will serve as the primary source for professional development workshops, and/or undergraduate and graduate classrooms. By focusing on social justice and multiculturalism as a broad construct, this volume has the potential to serve a wide variety of educational practitioners involved in the problem solving process.

Should the volume be chosen for use as a book-study or workshop, leaders will find the volume to be attractive in that it offers educators concrete and applied examples of problem solving in educational settings. The focus on strategies to enhance the problem solving efforts of school leaders provide the school leader practical source material for daily problem solving activities in school settings. The resources included in the text also support individual or team learning by providing opportunities for reflection on current practices as well as alternatives for future efforts.

Should the text be chosen as a primary or secondary text for classrooms, the text supports classes such as Multicultural Education, Organizational Leadership, School Culture and Governance and/or Decision Making, Curriculum and Instruction, and Policy and Law. The text is informed by knowledge of the ELCC/ISLLC standards for school leaders and a theoretical knowledge base. In this way, the text offers readers problem-solving strategies for daily practice within school contexts, linking theory to best practice in engaging and practical ways.

In summary, while some of the dimensions of school leadership and problem solving theory identified for examination in this volume can be found sprinkled here and there in the literature, no volume exists that identifies practical linkages between the two. The perspective assumed by this volume is different from both the decision making/data-based decision-making and school improvement literatures found in the field of educational leadership.

This volume is unique in that it offers not only strategies for organizational leadership and practice relative to the problem solving process, but also the potential for understanding and developing problem solving skills, which are of paramount importance for prospective and practicing school administrators.

PRACTICAL APPLICATIONS OF THIS VOLUME

There are many ways in which this volume may be used in classrooms and professional development seminars. The following are some suggestions, but it is recommended that facilitators of these cases use their personal pedagogical styles in the uses of the cases contained within this volume.

Pedagogical Suggestions:

1. Ideally, have students/participants read the case at home, asking them to take notes not only on the facts of the case, but also on their perceptions of the best course of action.
2. Assign additional resources (most cases have additional readings at the end) as homework when appropriate.
3. In a large group discussion, facilitating with a white board or chart paper, list the facts of the case as students/participants share their thoughts.
4. Ask clarifying questions and encourage debate about the facts among students/participants.
5. Break students/participants into small groups and have them answer the questions at the end of the case(s), and engage in additional activities as appropriate.
6. Share results of small group work as a large group discussion. Ask clarifying questions and encourage debate about among students/participants.
7. As a culminating whole group discussion, ask students/participants to identify the optimal course of action for all key actors in the case.

8. Additional work/homework. Ask students/participants to write a reflection on this experience. Adjust pedagogy based upon these responses.

As a follow-up to classroom discussion, students can be asked to write a case analysis and follow up with small group discussion to compare their analyses. To guide, students are recommended to follow some generic steps: 1) Identify the key actors and the role they play in this case study, 2) Identify the plot line—what happened? 3) What are the issues of this case? 4) Identify the causes and effects of each action. What actions (if any) served to escalate the situation? What actions (if any) served to remedy the situation? 5) What theory can you draw upon to explain what happened in this case? 6) What appropriate actions should be taken by the key actors in this case?

REFERENCES

Harvard Graduate School of Education (2013). Women in education leadership. *Programs in professional learning.* Cambridge, MA: Harvard Graduate School of Education.

Chapter One

"Discipline and Punish"

Racial Violence Breaks Out at the Alternative School

INTRODUCTION

This case explores how schools reproduce race and class inequality through discipline policies. Non-dominant students (students of color, i.e., persons primarily of African American and Latina/o ancestry who may also practice non-standard English language usage) often find themselves at odds with the culture of schools. Under these conditions, issues of misperceptions and proportionality become paramount.

With heightened anxiety over school safety and the advent of "zero tolerance" regulations, the possibility of unethical and unfair practices for students from poor and minority groups increases considerably. These severe policies mean that schools have an even greater obligation to make certain that rules are administered so that they do not further subjugate the most vulnerable segments of our population. The importance of viewing race and class in schools simultaneously and the problems associated with disciplinary reform are discussed in this case.

Often teachers are not privy to student backgrounds that would provide them with a frame of reference for why a particular student does not care about school, acts out, has issues with rage, and so on. Such is the case with Scott. Scott attends an alternative high school for students labeled "at-risk" for school failure. The most common reason students are sent to this school is behavioral infractions, for example, multiple suspensions, truancy, and the district policy that any student sentenced to a juvenile "lock-up," or detention center, return to the school district through the alternative school.

Many attendees at the alternative school have a history of truancy, drug and alcohol use, family problems, and thus have fallen behind their peers academically. Because many of these students have experienced large gaps in their educations, they may actively resist learning for fear of being ridiculed by more academically advanced peers or insensitive teaching practices.

THE CASE

The alternative high school currently provides services to approximately sixty adjudicated and non-adjudicated teens, behaviorally challenged adolescents, and other at-risk youth ages fourteen to twenty-one who are referred for placement through the district, Ohio Department of Job and Family Services, and other agencies throughout the state. The student body is comprised of 56.5 percent African American, 26 percent white, 8 percent multiracial, and 9.5 percent Hispanic students, with 15.6 percent labeled limited English proficiency. A large number of students (88.8 percent) are economically disadvantaged.

Central to its mission, the alternative school endeavors to "demonstrate sensitivity to the racial, cultural, ethical and religious backgrounds" of both staff and students.

Mr. Kohler is a white male in his early fifties who has been employed by the school for fifteen years, all of which he has spent at the alternative school in the role of principal. He hails from a rural area where he had previously taught for two years and was principal of an alternative school for another two years. Mr. Kohler holds a Master's degree and principal license. He has neither been trained in culturally responsive practices, nor has he advocated such training for his staff.

At the alternative school, 100 percent of the teachers are white. The alternative school, and the district in which it is a part, has had a majority white student population, approximately 65 percent to 70 percent. In recent years, as the district became more diverse, the alternative high school's level of diversity increased faster than the rate of the district; this is problematic, for a disproportionate number of African American students were being referred to the alternative school.

At the time of this case study, the African American student population at the alternative school was almost 50 percent. There was an overall unexamined privileging of whiteness throughout the district, which may have contributed to the disproportionate referrals of African American students to the alternative school. Teachers in the district have not received training on culturally responsive teaching practices. Multicultural education is not a core value and is not openly discussed.

While all teachers hold licensure in their teaching assignment, the faculty is young and inexperienced because of a high turnover rate. Teaching at the alternative school is a difficult assignment for a new teacher, and, after a year or two, most leave to fill other positions in the district's other two traditional high schools where the students have fewer academic and behavioral issues. Teachers reported leaving for more traditional teaching assignments because they did not feel they could make a difference, did not feel respected by the students or administration, and did not feel safe.

Another member of the staff is Arnie, the security guard. Arnie is a white male in his early fifties, has been employed by the school for two years, and has lived in the neighborhood surrounding the alternative school his entire life. Arnie does not have a background in education and has not been trained in culturally responsive practices.

Scott is a white male student at the alternative school, sent there directly from the middle school for "incorrigibility": failure to comply, lack of work completed, and courses passed; he is currently in his second year at the alternative school.

Colin is a white male student sent to the alternative school as a junior for repeated incidents of fighting and physical aggression, and various other infractions such as classroom disruption and disrespect of teachers. Colin had been known to tout racist hate speech in his classes and the hallways, and had been disciplined for it many times. This is his second year at the alternative school. Colin's grandmother is raising him while his mother works through a drug rehabilitation program. The identity of his father is unknown.

Ms. King is a white female in her late thirties working on her doctorate in urban education. She has sixteen years of experience teaching high school English and has worked at the alternative school for fourteen of those years. Ms. King is a believer in confronting the dominant social order. She is bright, thoughtful, and is there to make a difference.

During the first week of school in his second year at the alternative school, Scott completed an assignment in his English class for the first time. Usually, he would make comments under his breath, continually interrupting his teacher's directions with inappropriate comments or when listening to them in their entirety state, "This is stupid. I'm not doing this."

Usually, Scott's teacher, Ms. King, would have to ask him to leave so that she could focus her attention on the students who were there to learn, or the ones she could persuade to try. If she decided to ask him to leave, which was often, he would typically counter, "It's about time."

One day, somehow, Scott figured it out. Ms. King was so proud that he wrote a two-page essay in one hour that she did not question his request to go to the bathroom with only ten minutes of the period remaining. When Scott came back he was grumpy and despondent: he became the "old Scott" in a span of two minutes. "What happened?" Ms. King asked him. His shoulders slumped in response. She told him to sit at her desk, while she waited by the door until the bell rang.

When everyone filed out of the room at the sound of the bell, she asked him again. Scott replied, "Over the summer those new kids, Deshawn and Malik, tried to jump me. Now DeShawn's talking all kinds of stuff on Facebook. I told him to back the 'f' up. I don't care. I will 'f' him up right now. I don't care if we're on the bus. He starts talking shit, I'm done."

This reminded her of an incident last year, when she literally pushed a student out of her doorway who was trying to get to Scott and quickly slammed the door, holding Scott inside while pretending that was not what she was doing. "I gotta go," Scott grumbled.

The final bell had rung, and Scott made his way out of the building. Ms. King knew Scott. She knew that he would attempt to perform hyper-masculine behaviors; she knew that Scott's behavior would ideally end with a performance, without actually physically fighting, or by getting someone to fight for him. That was Scott's modus operandi.

Fighting is a common event in the hallways at the alternative school, and the males in the school were most commonly the participants. Deshawn is an African American student in ninth grade at the alternative school, sent directly from a juvenile detention facility per district policy. School faculty are not informed why students are sent to "lock-up." This is his first year at the alternative school.

Both parents work two jobs, and DeShawn is often the caregiver for his two younger siblings. Malik is an African American student at the alternative school, also sent there directly from a juvenile detention facility per district policy. Malik was sent to the juvenile detention facility because of multiple assault charges. This is also his first year at the alternative school, but he had been in no trouble at the school since his arrival one week prior.

Ms. King trailed a few feet behind Scott; down the hall she motioned to the principal in teacher sign that there could potentially be a problem and to come outside. As she was doing this, Scott motioned to his friend Colin. "You got my back, right?"

Uh oh, Ms. King thought.

As she reached the line of buses, Colin came into her peripheral vision; he took off his hoodie and ripped it to the ground. He crouched into a wrestling stance: legs in a stone plié, body bent into a forty-five degree angle, elbows partially bent, arms shaking; he closed his eyes as his rebel yell echoed off the yellow metal of the buses. Students hung from bus windows, jockeying for a front row seat.

Double uh oh, she thought.

Scott stood somewhere behind him, far out of the frame, as Colin confronted DeShawn and Malik. For Colin, it did not matter who started it, or if it was valid: a fight was a fight and that was good enough for him. But Scott was a posturer. Even though deep down he feared fighting, he needed to assert his masculinity. Colin was more than happy to be his stand-in, particularly when his foes were not white. Colin was known to be a white supremacist, and Ms. King worried that this conflict, not initially about race, would turn into a racial conflict now that Colin was involved.

As Colin confronted DeShawn, Malik, and another African American student, Malik stepped to him, and the two squared off. Arnie, the security guard, intervened, screaming about calling the police; he backed the three African American boys into the parking lot. The white boys, who gathered around Colin moments before, sans Scott, dispersed into the dwindling crowds and boarded various buses. The fight did not end that day; it evolved into something else, something much worse.

Ms. King stood and observed, looking around for the principal; she wondered what she should do now. Of the three African American boys that the security guard confronted in the parking lot, only DeShawn and Malik were involved in the initial conflict with Scott. The other boy was standing near Deshawn when the conflict ensued. The conflict between Scott, Deshawn, and Malik still needed to be resolved, as did the issues with Colin. But now there was also the issue with Arnie.

Ms. King noticed that the principal stood inside the main entrance door to the school, quietly monitoring students as they made their way through the halls and out to the buses. She looked at Mr. Kohler and pointed again toward the conflict. Ms. King was not sure if he did not see or just pretended not to see the conflict, or if his experience made him incapable of seeing the biased discipline that she saw. As the crowd dwindled, the principal turned around and walked into the office.

Ms. King, troubled by what she had witnessed, was certain that the administration would minimize the actions of the security guard in the parking lot. She decided to write everything down and speak to the principal the following morning.

The next day, Arnie entered the cafeteria before the bell rang signaling the start of the first class. Colin was standing alone along the wall surveying the scene, periodically banging his fists alternately against the wall behind him. Scott was not in attendance. Five African American boys, including Deshawn and Malik, sat together at a table toward the back of the room. Many students were in the cafeteria at that time, eating, talking, and milling around. There were five minutes left before the first warning bell. There was only one hallway for the sixty students who attended.

Arnie walked directly over to the table of African American males and told them that they had one minute to disperse. Deshawn stood up angrily, and shouted, "Why are you picking on us? We are just sitting here. We didn't *do* anything! Why don't you say something to that psycho over there" [indicating Colin, still pounding his fists and gazing menacingly at their table].

"I don't have to explain anything to you," Arnie replied, "now move!"

"Make us!" Malik shouted. Upon Malik's announcement, all the boys crossed their arms and looked expectantly at Arnie.

As the first warning bell rang, Mr. Kohler entered the cafeteria and immediately noticed the tension escalating at the back of the room. After having many conversations with Ms. King about the racial tensions in the school, Mr. Kohler was unsure with how to proceed with Ms. King's concerns about the inequality of discipline problems along racial lines at his school.

TEACHING NOTES

School administrators are obligated to avoid and redress racial discrimination in the administration of student discipline. Title IV of the Civil Rights Act of 1964 (Title IV), 42 U.S.C. §§ 2000c et seq. prohibits discrimination in public elementary and secondary schools based on race, color, or national origin, among other bases. Federal law also prohibits discriminatory discipline based on other factors, including disability, religion, and sex.

Since 1968, the federal government has collected civil rights data about schools and whether equal educational opportunities are afforded all students. These data provide critical information to the U.S. Department of Education on enforcing federal civil rights laws.

Racial disparities in school discipline policies are well documented among older students, but actually begin during preschool and contribute to the school-to-prison pipeline. Young men and boys of color are disproportionately affected by suspensions and zero tolerance policies in schools, and consequently are less likely to graduate on time and more likely to be suspended again. They are also more likely to repeat a grade, drop out, and become involved in the juvenile justice system.

Although African American students represent 15 percent of students, they make up 35 percent of students suspended once, 44 percent of those suspended more than once, and 36 percent of students expelled (U.S. Department of Education, 2015). Further, over 50 percent of students who were involved in school-related arrests or referred to law enforcement are Hispanic or Black (U.S. Department of Education, 2015).

The school-to-prison pipeline contributes to the atmosphere of increased surveillance of schools, including police presence in schools, zero tolerance policies, physical restraint tactics, and automatic consequence policies, resulting in suspensions from school (Alexander, 2012; Tate et al., 2014). Subject to disproportionate numbers of behavior referrals, students of color are more negatively impacted by these policies than their white counterparts (Alexander, 2012; Tate et al., 2014).

Juveniles of color are also perceived differently by the justice system than their white counterparts; prosecutors tend to attribute white criminal behavior to external factors, whereas criminal behavior exhibited by youth of color is often attributed to internal factors such as personality flaws and/or disrespect (Alexander, 2012; Goff, Jackson, Lewis Di Leone, Culotta, & DiTomasso, 2014; Tate, et al., 2014). Because of these factors, viewing race, class, and gender in schools simultaneously and the problems associated with disciplinary reform in education is critical.

The phenomenon of the school-to-prison pipeline leads to more students being introduced to the criminal justice system, and, ultimately, more juveniles being incarcerated. The increasing use of disciplinary sanctions such as in-school and out-of-school suspensions, expulsions, or referrals to law enforcement authorities creates the potential for negative educational outcomes and can contribute to the school to prison pipeline.

There seems to be a connection between exclusionary discipline policies and practices that diminishes educational engagement, decreased academic achievement, increased behavior problems, increased likelihood of dropping out, substance abuse, and involvement with juvenile justice systems. Fair and equitable discipline policies are an important component of creating an environment where all students feel safe and welcome.

Colorblind and colormute ideologies condemn any words or language that may relate, signify, or give meaning to race; in reality, it perpetuates racism, denials of institutional or structural inequality, and the myth of meritocracy. Critical Race Theory (CRT) challenges this through counter-narratives that build awareness of the reality of racism. To be anti-racist, we need to not only acknowledge racism, but also to acknowledge people's lived experiences.

When given the opportunity to talk about race in schools, students can have salient conversations (Pollock, 2004). However, students are not often given these opportunities in schools. In their research detailing the consequences of the dehumanization of Black children, Goff, Jackson, Di Leone, Culotta, and DiTomasso (2014) found that Black boys are perceived as older and less "innocent" than their same age white peers, more culpable for their actions, and thus more appropriate targets for police violence.

According to Ladson-Billings (2009), CRT involves academic achievement, socio-political consciousness, and cultural competence. Because CRT seeks, through education, to identify, problematize, and ultimately transform institutions and society with the goal of ending all forms of oppression, culturally responsive teachers must not only possess the will to end oppression but the *knowledge* to inform their choices and actions.

The main principles of CRT include the recognition of race and racism in society, a critique of the traditional western values of objectivity and neutrality, a reliance on the knowledge and experience of people of color in the definition of its tenants, an interdisciplinary focus, the goal of the elimination of all form of oppression (Lynn, 1999), and, we would argue, CRT necessitates the advocacy of anti-racist whites.

Because CRT seeks to determine how racism is perpetuated, for the purposes of undermining racial bias within systems and institutions, dismantling white privilege is a necessary component of this mission. This necessitates the cooperation of white allies. By extension, critical race pedagogy seeks, through education, to identify, problematize, and ultimately transform institutions and society with the goal of ending all forms of oppression. According to Ladson-Billings (2009), teachers must study their students in order to decide what and how to teach.

Culturally responsive pedagogy (Gay, 2010) runs parallel to CRT because it requires educators to possess the will to end oppression and the *knowledge* to inform their choices and actions. Howard (2006) defines "responsiveness" as dealing with "Our capacity as teachers to know and connect with the actual lived experience, personhood, and learning modalities of the students who are in our classroom" (p. 131). Culturally responsive educators take the time to research the experiences, individuality, and learning styles of students to better reach/teach them by meeting them where they live.

Anti-racist pedagogy involves selecting culturally responsive curriculum, problematizing the curriculum, engaging in conversations about students' lived experiences, engaging in social and political critique, problematizing one's privilege and standpoint, and facilitating critical thinking. In this sense, education can serve the cause of liberation: students and teachers working together to claim an education that does not undermine personal identity.

In order for youth to transform their lives, they must understand the oppressive forces that impact them and their communities and possess the ability to relate to other oppressed groups in order to engage in transformational social action (Flores-Gonzales, Rodriguez, & Rodriguez-Muniz, 2006). Youth labeled "at-risk" are often subject to what Valenzuela (1999) deems "subtractive schooling," which strips youth of their particular social and cultural resources by devaluing their linguistic and cultural backgrounds and, by extension, their appearance, mannerisms, and styles of speech; views them as operating from intellectual deficits; and thus often funnels them into basic skills programs (Hallman, 2009). Counter-narratives can counteract dominant and negative portrayals of students labeled "at-risk," and of students with non-dominant linguistic and cultural backgrounds (that are often viewed as one and the same).

QUESTIONS FOR DISCUSSION

1. Based on the facts of this case, are some students made to feel more welcome within the school than others? Explain your thoughts.
2. What are the issues pertaining to leadership in this school that should be addressed?
3. What steps should be taken by the principal, Mr. Kohler, to promote a positive and healthy culture in this school?
4. In your interpretation of the facts of this case, are there differential expectations for students based on race? If so, what should be done about them from a leadership perspective? If not, defend your position.
5. What should the principal do to support teachers like Ms. King?
6. After taking into consideration the differential referral procedures on a district basis that result in African American students being referred to the alternative school, what should the principal do? The district?
7. How should Ms. King proceed with her concerns about the inequality of discipline problems along racial lines at his school?
8. What are some effective interventions that could be designed to promote more culturally responsive practices within the school that include students, parents, support staff, educators, agency liaisons, and the local community?
9. What, if anything, should the administration do about the behavior of Arnie, the security guard?

ADDITIONAL ACTIVITIES

Activity 1

Review the following two documents:

U.S. Department of Education Office for Civil Rights. (2014, March). *Civil rights data collection, data snapshot: school discipline.* http://ocrdata.ed.gov/Downloads/CRDC-School-Discipline-Snapshot.pdf.

U.S. Department of Education. (2015, July). *Educators gather at the white house to rethink school discipline.* http://www.ed.gov/news/press-releases/educators-gather-white-house-rethink-school-discipline.

Based upon your reading, does your interpretation of the facts of the case change in any way?

Activity 2

Review the following scholarly article:

Goff, P. A., Jackson, M. C., Di Leone, B. A., Culotta, C. M., & DiTomasso, N. A. (2014). The essence of innocence: Consequences of dehumanizing black children. *Journal of Personality and Social Psychology.* http://dx.doi.org/10.1037/a0035663.

Based upon your reading, how does the dehumanization of Black and Brown students factor into this case?

Activity 3

Read the U.S. Departments of Education and Justice guidelines to school districts on zero-tolerance policies and discipline tactics:http://www2.ed.gov/policy/gen/guid/school-discipline/guiding-principles.pdf.
These guidelines provide a powerful example of the federal government using data to take action to bolster outcomes and reduce disparities for minority students. Divide participants into two groups and have them debate the pros and cons of zero-tolerance policies and discipline tactics.

Activity 4

Develop a comprehensive, appropriate, culturally responsive, and effective program demonstrated to 1) reduce disruption and misconduct, 2) support and reinforce positive behavior and character development, and 3) help students succeed.

Activity 5

Use real school data on discipline, including suspension and expulsion rates and race, to identify gaps and cases of discrimination using the National Center for Education Statistics (http://nces.ed.gov/pubs2010/2010015/indicator4_17.asp). Discuss methods to ensure equal access to educational opportunities. Identify strategies to reduce misbehavior and maintain a safe learning environment, including conflict resolution, restorative practices, counseling, and structured systems of positive interventions.

Activity 6

Research conducted by Epstein and Sheldon (2002) indicates that regardless of schools' prior rates of discipline, the more family and community involvement activities were implemented, the fewer students were disciplined by being sent to principals' offices or given detention or in-school suspension. Activities for two types of involvement, parenting and volunteering, were most predictive of reducing the percentages of students who were subject to discipline. Also, schools that improved the quality of their partnership programs reported fewer students in need of discipline. Identify methods of creating more connections and greater cooperation among the school, family, and community contexts as a way for schools to improve student behavior and school discipline.

REFERENCES

ACE Reporter. (2003). Origins and essence of the study. *ACE Reporter, 1*(1), 1–4. http://acestudy.org/yahoo_site_admin/assets/docs/ARV1N1.127150541.pdf.

Alexander, M. (2012). *The new Jim Crow: Mass incarceration in the age of colorblindness.* New York, NY: The New Press.

Epstein, J. L. & Sheldon, S. B. (2002). Presented and accounted for: Improving student attendance through family and community involvement. *Journal of Educational Research, 95,* 308–18.

Felitti, V. J., Anda, R. F., Nordenberg, D., Williamson, D. F., Spitz, A. M., Edwards, V., & Koss, M. P. (1998). The relationship of adult health status to childhood abuse and household dysfunction. *American Journal of Preventive Medicine, 14,* 245–58.

Flores-Gonzales, N., Rodriguez, M., & Rodriguez-Muniz, M. (2006). From hip-hop to humanization: Batey urbano as a space for latino youth culture and community action. In S. Ginwright, P. Noguera, & J. Cammarota (Eds.)., *Beyond resistance! Youth activism and community change: New democratic possibilities for practice and policy for america's youth* (pp. 175–96). New York: Routledge.

Hallman, H. L. (2009). "Dear Tupac, you speak to me": Recruiting hip hop as curriculum at a school for pregnant and parenting teens. *Equity and Excellence in Education, 42*(1), 36–51.

Howard, G. R. (2006). *We can't teach what we don't know. White teachers, multiracial schools* (2nd ed.). New York, NY: Teachers College Press.

Gay, G. (2010). *Culturally responsive teaching: Theory, research, and practice* (2nd ed.). New York, NY: Teachers College Press.

Goff, P. A., Jackson, M. C., Di Leone, B. A., Culotta, C. M., & DiTomasso, N. A. (2014). The essence of innocence: Consequences of dehumanizing black children. *Journal of Personality and Social Psychology.* http://dx.doi.org/10.1037/a0035663.

Ladson-Billings, G. (2009). *The dreamkeepers: Successful teachers of African American children* (2nd ed.). San Francisco, CA: Jossey-Bass.

Lynn, M. (1999). Toward a critical race pedagogy: A research note. *Urban Education, 33*(5), 606–26.

Pollock (2004). *Colomute: Race talk dilemmas in an American school.* Princeton, NJ: Princeton University Press.

Tate, W. F., Hamilton, C., Jones, B. D., Robertson, W. B., Macrander, A., Schultz, L., & Thorne-Wallington, E. (2014). Serving vulnerable children and youth in the urban context. In H. R. Milner & K. Lomotey (Eds.), *Handbook of urban education* (pp. 3–23). New York, NY: Routledge.

U.S. Department of Education Office for Civil Rights. (2014, March). *Civil rights data collection, data snapshot: school discipline.* Retrieved from http://ocrdata.ed.gov/ Downloads/CRDC-School-Discipline-Snapshot.pdf.

U.S. Department of Education. (2015). *Civil rights data collection.* http://www2.ed.gov/about/offices/list/ocr/data.html.

U.S. Department of Education. (2015, July). *Educators gather at the white house to rethink school discipline.* http://www.ed.gov/news/press-releases/educators-gather-white-house-rethink-school-discipline.

Valenzuela, A. (1999). *Subtractive schooling: U.S. Mexican youth and the politics of caring.* New York, NY: State University of New York Press

Chapter Two

Pink is for Girls

A Case of Single-Sex Education

INTRODUCTION

Because most teachers and educational leaders are not also researchers, the field of education is rife with faddism. Some authors and proponents of educational reform are quick to take advantage of this fact. This case challenges the reader to sift through proposed educational solutions to the pressing problems faced in classrooms and schools for their veracity and make evidence based decisions. Some researchers would argue that single-sex education is a current educational fad, and one that is not research based.

In the 1996 case *United States v. Virginia*, the U.S. Supreme Court ruled on the constitutionality of single-sex public education. Single-sex education in public schools was ruled constitutional when comparable courses, services, and facilities are made available to both sexes. The proliferation of single-sex schools began in the 2000s, after President George W. Bush weakened Title IX provisions in 2006 allowing for expanded sex segregation in schools.

Proponents of single-sex education argue that there are differences in how boys and girls learn and behave in educational settings and further the notion that separating boys and girls, by classrooms or schools, increases students' achievement and academic interest. Proponents of single-sex education argue that by separating the sexes, teachers are better able to meet the needs of each student because students are not distracted by the "opposite" sex and can pay closer attention to the lesson. Opponents of single-sex education argue that segregation leads to increased stereotyping and limited social skills.

Neuroscientist and opponent of single-sex education Lise Eliot examined decades of research on neuroplasticity and found that infant brains are highly malleable and that parents and educators impose their own gender biases upon infants and young children, further impacting their future educational development.

Single-sex programs and schools, women's colleges for example, created for affirmative purposes, such as redressing past discriminations, were permissible under the original intent of Title IX. However, the expansion of single-sex education in the post-Bush era for non-affirmative purposes not only flies in the face of the spirit of Title IX, but also serves to promote traditional gender roles, and contributes to the backlash against egalitarianism in education.

The Department of Education's Office for Civil Rights has, at the time of this writing (August 2015), closed investigations of complaints against single-sex classrooms as violations of Title IX in Wisconsin after schools ceased the practice. Many other complaints of sex discrimination and Title IX violations are still under investigation in Florida, Texas, and Idaho.

This case is both timely and relevant to teachers and educational leaders, for it highlights the importance of using evidence to inform district decisions, particularly as decisions related to learning become standard practice. Educational leaders must also understand the need to engage their staff in relevant and research based professional development in order to build the organizational capacity needed to support student success.

Collaboration and implementation of a shared vision and mission facilitates this process. In this case, the curriculum director, Mr. Cooper, has developed a plan for curriculum changes in which boys and girls would be separated by classroom, and participate in distinct curriculums based on the premise that innate differences between boys and girls should drive educational models and instructional strategies designed to address the needs and strengths of each sex. The reader is asked to decide if this plan is not only scientifically valid, but also the best decision for this particular school.

THE CASE

Mr. Chambers was excited to begin his new job as a third grade teacher at Roosevelt Elementary. A twenty-four-year old recent graduate of a prestigious university in New York City, he accepted a job in a midwestern suburb quite near to an urban setting after a few phone interviews and a lucrative offer.

Mr. Chambers was excited to leave the stress of New York for a slower paced community. He was also excited to get in on the ground floor of new programs within the school that were being piloted. Mr. Chambers is a white male is his mid-twenties. Based upon his pre-service teacher education program, Mr. Chambers is aware that the single-sex curriculum is not based upon scientific research or best practices. Although not 100 percent clear on the details, he was told that the third grade curriculum was in the process of being revamped based upon recent neuroscience findings. He was assured that he would be apprised of the details upon his arrival, one month prior to the start of the school year. He was also promised that he would be involved in all curricular transitions.

Roosevelt Elementary, founded in 1936, is a suburban-rural public school, kindergarten through grade five, situated in an upper middle class area. The school is home to classrooms, a gymnasium, a visual arts studio, a theatre, and athletic fields. Enrollment is approximately 350 students. Roosevelt employs twenty-three full and part-time faculty members, of which seventeen have a Master's degree or higher, including two PhDs.

Roosevelt Elementary is known for its academic excellence, scoring an overall "A" on the state report card for the last five academic years and has met all indicators. The school earned an "A" on the performance index, which measures the achievement of every student and on its overall value added, which measures the growth of all students. The school also earned an "A" for gifted students, an "A" for disabled students, and a "C" for students in the lowest 20 percent. The data indicated that a large percentage of third grade boys were underperforming their female counterparts in reading.

Students who have test scores in the lowest 20 percent in the state was an alarming finding to the school. The principal explained, "That group needs our continued attention and focus. We need to find a way to reach those students and provide the education they need. We need to provide the latest in teaching strategies and curriculum." Roosevelt Elementary's curricular goals require many approaches. To meet the needs of the students, several key approaches to learning in particular distinguish the curriculum: more classroom time devoted to literacy, and gender differentiated classrooms and instruction in third grade.

It was last spring when the curriculum director together with the principal of Roosevelt Elementary brought to the school board's attention research-based findings on the effects of differentiating the curriculum by student sex. Through the use of curriculum differentiation by sex, school authorities could make decisions that affect how and how much a student learns. The rationale for organizing the curriculum on the basis of sex was presented as a method of facilitating the instruction of the academic population and to manage their behavior. Before the end of the academic year, the school board adopted a policy of differentiating the school curriculum by sex.

Mr. Chambers's move went smoothly. He was able to secure an apartment halfway between the suburban school and the city. He purchased a car, traveled across the country, and quickly moved into his new community. On

August 1, Mr. Chambers entered his new place of employment, Roosevelt Elementary, for new faculty orientation. Upon entering the building, Mr. Chambers was welcomed by two older men who shepherded him into a conference room, where he was asked to take a seat.

A few moments later, the orientation began. Mr. Chambers looked around and noticed that there were no women in the room. This surprised him because he knew that women typically made up the majority of the teaching force, particularly in elementary education.

Over the course of Roosevelt Elementary history, there had been decades of academic success. However, in a changing educational climate, Roosevelt is a microcosm of the many challenging issues and trends in the field of education today.

To clarify, changes in state level legislation require students to be on track for reading success by the end of third grade. This involves the identification of students from kindergarten through grade three that are behind in reading to make sure they receive the help and support they need. As a result of these and other changes from the state Department of Education, administrators at Roosevelt Elementary felt curriculum changes were necessary.

Mr. Lawrence, curriculum director for the district, began the orientation presentation by disseminating two books to each participant: *Boys and Girls Learn Differently! A Guide for Teachers and Parents*, by Michael Gurian, and *Why Gender Matters: What Parents and Teachers Need to Know about the Emerging Science of Sex Differences*, by Leonard Sax. Sax's National Association for Choice in Education and Gurian's Gurian Institute are the two foremost organizations that have worked to spread single-sex education throughout the country (Cohen & Levit, 2013).

Mr. Lawrence is a white male in his late forties. A veteran of the district, he has spent his entire career at Roosevelt Elementary and has been unhappy with the relative lack of success of the boys in the school in comparison with the girls. He recently attended a professional development seminar entitled "The Boy Crisis in Education." Mr. Lawrence has repeatedly stated that he wanted his classroom to be "girl-free" because girls tend to be "bossy."

Mr. Lawrence had developed a plan for curriculum changes at Roosevelt Elementary and Principal Brock fully endorsed his implementation plan. Dr. Brock is a relatively new hire to the district. She is in her third year as principal of Roosevelt Elementary. Roosevelt Elementary is the most under-performing school in the district. Although the school is not in danger of being placed in academic emergency, Dr. Brock is under pressure to improve test scores, particularly in third grade because of the state's new provisions with the Third Grade Reading Guarantee.

Mr. Lawrence then began his PowerPoint presentation where he demon-strated the third grade curricular plan for the year: boys and girls would be separated by classroom, and participate in distinct curriculums based on the premise that innate differences between boys and girls should drive educational models and instructional strategies designed to address the needs and strengths of each sex.

Mr. Lawrence opened his presentation by citing a recent online article from *Time* magazine written by Christina Hoff Sommers. Mr. Lawrence went on to discuss the views outlined in the article, such as: classrooms educating boys should be based on action, activity, engagement, and fun; and boys should not be expected to sit still and be quiet, but should be free to explore their "maleness" in a non-judgmental environment.

Mr. Lawrence argued that the teachers of the boys would amplify their voices electronically based upon inherently male "hearing deficiencies," as delineated by Leonard Sax. Boys would also be exposed to a logic-centered, inquiry based math curriculum, which would take precedence over the traditional literacy-based elementary curriculum.

After an hour-long presentation detailing what boys could expect within this "male-centered" curriculum, including constructivist principles such as inquiry and project-based learning, learning through play, non-authoritarian behavioral expectations, student-centered literacy centers, etc., Mr. Chambers wondered, not only, where the women teachers were, but also what the curriculum for the girls would be like. He wondered if he should ask such a question on his first day. He decided he would bide his time.

After an hour-long presentation and another hour of discussion of proposed literature for the male curriculum based on themes such as sports, hunting, fishing, war, scouting, and pets, Mr. Chambers was released for a twenty-minute break.

He removed himself from the conference room into the adjoining staff room for some coffee, and felt relieved when he noticed a table of women chatting. He asked the table of his future colleagues if he could join them. They happily obliged. Mr. Chambers introduced himself. The four women at the table introduced themselves, two of them were veteran second grade teachers, and the other two were also new hires working in the third grade. Mr. Chambers asked the two new hires what texts they were provided and what they thought of their curriculum presentation.

The two women noted that they were given the same texts as Mr. Chambers. They both indicated that they were unimpressed with the curricular presentation. Ms. Stanley is a white female in her mid-twenties. Based upon her pre-service teacher education program, Ms. Stanley is aware of the provisions of Title IX that prohibit sex segregation and also of the "pseudo-scientific" proliferations of traditional gender role/sex segregated curricula. Ms. Stanley indicated that the curriculum as presented was no different from what she herself had experienced as a young girl in the 1990s, "The girls are expected to sit in rows, to raise their hands when speaking, to speak in quiet voices, and to focus on their inherent strengths: reading and writing."

Ms. Stanley smiled shyly. The other women said nothing. After a pregnant pause, time was called on the break and all were asked to return to their respective rooms. As Mr. Chambers and Ms. Stanley parted ways, she whispered, "I was told that this new curriculum would be progressive and based upon neuroscience. I am pretty sure everything I learned in my teacher preparation program in terms of best practices is falling on its face, but I am afraid to speak up."

Mr. Chambers went back to his orientation and found more of the same: the separation of sexes not only of the students, but also of the staff. He was surprised that there were so many male teachers in the school to teach the male students, as he knew this was not the norm. He was dismayed by the binary views of gender that seemed to be held by the current staff and administration and justified by the texts that were passed out at the orientation. A small portion of the presentation was used to provide information on what would be occurring in the girls' classes.

The changes, as advocated by Mr. Lawrence, included increasing structure for boys through play and connection for girls through quiet communication. Nerf baseball bats were given to boys in order to release tension, and books with strong male characters who take action were strongly recommended. Teachers were encouraged to allow girls to take their shoes off to decrease stress, and to give them manipulatives, especially in the science classes.

It was also noted that girls would be provided with fuzzy pastel pink sweaters because they are more likely than boys to feel cold. For spelling and vocabulary lessons incorporating physical activity, girls would be provided hula hoops and small rubber balls. The boys would be provided with yo-yos, bats, and badminton rackets.

After the orientation ended, all staff members were shepherded into the gym for a "welcome back" presentation by the school principal, Dr. Brock. Dr. Brock welcomed the new teachers by introducing all by name and inviting them to stand when called. She then expressed her enthusiasm for the newly devised single-sex curriculum that would be piloted for the third grade classes.

She then thanked Mr. Lawrence for his work on this issue and for introducing this innovative idea to the school. She stated that she was inspired to make these changes after having conversations with Mr. Lawrence about how boys are being short changed when it comes to instructional strategies employed in the classroom. As evidence for this sentiment, she cited the current media blitz about the "boy crisis" in education.[1]

Historically speaking, this is nothing new. In the early 1900s, the boy crisis was a portent that constant interaction with women in school was robbing young men of their manhood (Maschke, 1997). Dr. Brock indicated that the effectiveness of this new pilot would be studied for potential extension into all grades at the elementary school.

Dr. Brock then invited Mr. Lawrence to the stage, who subsequently extolled the virtues of their new adopted single-sex curricula, which, he argued, would elevate all students' reading scores and literacy experiences in general because boys would be reading about boys' experiences in an environment that actively engaged boys' natural abilities through elevated teacher voice, competition, and active performance of literary text.

Girls would be reading about experiences that were paradigmatic of girls' experiences in an environment that was dimly lit, quiet, and safe, where girls would feel comfortable raising their hands, as they tend to do, and to share their points of view without being "shouted down" by male voices.

Mr. Chambers listened intently to the presentation while looking around to try to gauge the perceptions of his new colleagues. He did not get much of a sense of his new colleagues' opinions of the curricular changes one way or the other. Dr. Brock returned to the microphone when Mr. Lawrence finished speaking and announced that new faculty would now remain in the auditorium where they would meet their mentors. Mr. Chambers was soon introduced to Ms. Blankenship.

Ms. Blankenship is a woman in her mid-forties, and a fifteen-year veteran of Roosevelt Elementary. She is the only teacher of color at Roosevelt Elementary and one of only a few in the entire district. Ms. Blankenship has been an outspoken critic of the single-sex experiment at Roosevelt Elementary, and despite providing evidence to support her counter-arguments, her claims were largely ignored.

Mr. Chambers was relieved to find that the single-sex experiment did not extend to faculty mentoring. Ms. Blankenship offered to give Mr. Chambers a tour of the school, where he quickly learned that there were simply not enough veteran male teachers to be paired with the number of new male hires.

During the tour, Mr. Chambers learned that Ms. Blankenship was a fifteen-year veteran of the school with a specialization in project-based learning. He was pleased to learn that they shared many common pedagogical strategies and were philosophically aligned. As they neared the end of their tour, Ms. Blankenship suggested they grab coffee and then continue their chat in Mr. Chambers' classroom, which he had yet to see.

Ms. Blankenship escorted Mr. Chambers to his classroom and proceeded to explain various school policies and procedures. Then the two sat down at a table in the back of the classroom. "So," Ms. Blankenship began, "what did you think of today?"

Mr. Chambers smiled. "Well, I am not exactly sure. I have to tell you. I am a bit surprised about the curricular changes that are taking place this year. Since you have been here a while, what do you think?"

Ms. Blankenship hesitated, and then smiled, "Do you really want to know?"

"More than you know," he replied.

Ms. Blankenship smiled again, "How much time have you got?" Ms. Blankenship continued cautiously, "I am very concerned about the teaching of stereotypes. This reminds me a lot of separate but equal, and we well know that was nowhere near equal. I know that girls like to yell and play too. I have seen similar experiments such as this in urban communities, but in those communities, the goal is to exert maximum control. But, I am still suspicious. This seems like just another fad.

Education is rife with them. My mentor once told me, 'if you do not like something that is occurring in education, just wait it out—because it will change.' The change process can be one of trepidation for many, and, often-times, teachers are resistant to change. Some may not feel that a particular change is important despite any data provided to convince them otherwise. Many will not change what they do in the classroom.

The problem is we don't have enough scholars within our ranks, so the decisions that affect us, but more importantly, those that affect our kids, come from the expertise of the curriculum director, Mr. Lawrence. But, enough negativity. Since this affects you directly, I suggest that you just observe, study, and measure. We can change things."

Mr. Chambers went home that night to peruse the texts he was given and to reformulate the lesson plans that he had been working on all summer to accommodate some of these single-sex mandates. Although he was happy to have been assigned a mentor he felt he could trust, he was not as optimistic as he thought he would be beginning the first school year of his teaching career. He never imagined that a philosophy that he did not agree with would be imposed on him. Although he felt intellectually prepared to speak out, he was fearful for his job.

Discouraged at the prospect of working on a curriculum that he did not believe in, Mr. Chambers decided to do some research on his own. He logged onto his computer and began reading peer reviewed articles on neuroscience and sex differences. He soon came upon the following, "Our actual ability differences are quite small. Although psychologists can measure statistically significant distinctions between large groups of men and women or boys and girls, there is much more overlap in the academic and even social-emotional abilities of the genders than there are differences. . . . [T]he range of perfor-mance within each gender is wider than the difference between the average boy and girl" (Eliot, 2010, pp. 32-33). In the article Mr. Chambers read, neuroscientist Eliot argues that there appears to be a difference between females and males in academic progress as indicated by differences in test scores on the National Assessment of Educational Progress (NAEP) in every year of the assessment since 1971 (Eliot, 2010; U.S. Department of Education, 2005). As Eliot argues, there is a small gap with females outperforming males in reading and males outperforming females in math.

Similar gaps between females and males exist on the Program for International Student Assessment (PISA) (Else-Quest, Hyde, & Linn, 2010). However, as Eliot argues, a closer examination reveals that the gaps vary significantly by age, ethnicity, and nationality (Eliot, 2010). Interestingly, a recent analysis of PISA data found that higher female performance in math is correlated with higher levels of gender equity in various countries (Eliot, 2010). Mr. Chambers wondered just how harmful the single-sex education at Roosevelt Elementary would be for girls' math scores.

Mr. Chambers continued his reading, limiting his searches to only peer reviewed journals, and found the overwhelming sentiments were similar to Eliot's. He wondered why his field was so vulnerable to education fads as opposed to examining and utilizing scientific research. He went to bed troubled and angry. Sleeping little, he pondered what he should do with the information he had gathered that evening.

The next day, Mr. Chambers returned to work for a day of planning and classroom set up. He did not yet have a plan to broach any of the information he had gleaned the night before with any of his colleagues, but he was happy when Ms. Stanley appeared in the door of his classroom first thing. After exchanging brief pleasantries, Ms. Stanley, nodding toward the door of the classroom asked, "Do you mind if I shut this?"

"Please," Mr. Chambers responded and took a seat, offering Ms. Stanley a chair across from his.

"I did a little bit of research last night on single-sex classrooms and schools across the country," she paused. She continued when Mr. Chamber's wry smile and nod of the head confirmed to her that she was safe. "I found that the American Civil Liberties Union is characterizing programs like ours as sex discrimination. They are winning cases all over the country. I do not feel comfortable with this curriculum. I am not sure what I can do about this, but I knew that I had to talk to someone. We could go to the union about this, but neither of us have tenure. I am afraid of being characterized as a 'trouble maker.'"

"We share the same boat," Mr. Chambers relied. "I too did some research last night, but my angle was on the examination of the purported science behind these decisions. I found that there is no scientific justification for this curriculum. In fact, the science indicates quite the opposite. I do not have any ideas on what we should do."

The two in silence for a moment before Ms. Stanley stated, "How about this: what if we write a report, I'll take the legal angle and you take the science angle. We can put our two pieces together, and then figure out what to do." The two agreed that they would come together the next day and put the pieces of their report together.

At the end of the following day, Mr. Chambers and Ms. Stanley compiled their report and brainstormed what to do. Mr. Chambers broached an idea, "You know, I think we should bring Ms. Blankenship in on this. She is a veteran teacher, and a critic of faddism."

"Do you trust her?" Ms. Stanley inquired.

"I do," Mr. Blankenship replied.

"Then let's do it," Ms. Stanley smiled. Mr. Chambers walked to the phone and dialed the classroom of Ms. Blankenship. When she answered, Mr. Chambers asked if Ms. Blankenship would come down to his classroom.

When Ms. Blankenship arrived, the two presented their report to her and waited for a response. Ms. Blankenship smiled as she read the report. When she was finished, she looked up. "I just have one consideration that neither of you have broached in your report. You do not mention the issue of where a transgender child would fit within these third-grade classrooms. Statistically speaking, this is likely to happen. Now, where is this child going to fit? Other than this issue that we definitely need to address, I am on board. How can I help?"

TEACHING NOTES

Education is rife with faddism, as indicated in the statement, "if you do not like something that is occurring in education, just wait it out—because it will change." Some authors and proponents of educational change are quick to take advantage of the fact that most educators are not researchers and peddle solutions that are not research based to provide "quick fix" solutions to the problems faced by school personnel today. In order to truly address the issues associated with accountability and educational reform, the educational system requires strong organizational structures guided by effective leaders. Whether a new intervention program or instructional method or another innovation, the starting point for any change is a clear vision.

Vision is representative of the values and culture of a school (Kaufman, Herman, & Watters, 1996, p. 49). It gives leaders substance and makes them stand for something worth following—a widely shared purpose or vision (Boyd, 1992).

Warren Bennis and Burt Nanus (2007) wrote:

> Leaders articulate and define what has previously remained implicit or unsaid; then they invent images, metaphors, and models that provide a focus for new attention. By so doing, they consolidate or challenge prevailing wisdom. In short, an essential factor in leadership is the capacity to influence and organize meaning for the members of the organization (p. 59).

Vision provides a picture or mental image of an organization's direction or desired future and guides the work of the organization—it is a desire to see improvement.

Educational leaders must understand the principles for the development, articulation, implementation, and stewardship of a district vision of learning (ELCC, 2011, p. 7). The leader is the person who uses vision to bring order, definition, and direction that helps others make sense of the bigger picture (Sergiovanni, 2001). The leaders actions symbolize the vision and helps teachers make sense of it.

Strategic leadership is the process whereby leaders engage their communities in shaping their views and to focus everyone's attention and energy on specific goals. The mission of a district is a general statement indicating a desired condition or destination towards, which the district or personnel in the district strive to realize or attain through collective and individualized actions.

Stewardship is a concept advanced by Robert Greenleaf, who believed that the best way to lead was by serving. "Stewardship involves using foresight: employing power ethically; seeking consensus in-group decisions, where possible; and envisioning leadership as employing persuasion and building relationships based on trust" (Frick, 2004, pp. 338–345). The way that power is distributed is shaped by who is making the decisions and who is being affected. Power over is when one person makes a decision that affects another and power with is when a group of people are involved in making decisions. Power with requires an agreement to act in a manner that serves the group. Power with helps establish trust within an organization, buy-in to the innovation, and clear direction (Nyberg, 1981).

To exercise stewardship, leaders must have knowledge of how to develop a broadly shared vision and mission to guide district decisions and to support change at the school level (Fullan & Miles, 1992; Louis, Leithwood, Wahlstrom & Anderson, 2010; Spillane & Thompson, 1997), and knowledge of how to develop trust as a requisite variable in shared visioning and school improvement (Louis & Kruse, 1995; Spillane & Thompson, 1997). A leader and followers should hold a shared set of values and commitment that bond them together in a common cause to work toward a common goal (Sergiovanni, 2001).

Organizational vision should be developed collaboratively with a clear understanding of an organization's current reality. Principals should involve the whole staff in developing a vision for accomplishing goals and in creating a practical plan to achieve goals. According to Boisot (1995), "When knowledge is drawn together in this way and applied to areas of professional practice, such as the curriculum, learning, teaching, organizational behavior, and leadership, the result is the formation of intuitively formed patterns or gestalt" (p. 36). A widely shared sense of purpose or vision accompanied by broad-based involvement in decision making, especially decisions regarding teaching and learning and curricular issues, is crucial to change efforts.

Leaders must also know how to use evidence to inform district decisions, particularly as decisions related to learning become standard practice (Fullan, 1985). Effective policy implementers understand the importance of maintaining continuity with existing beliefs and practices and developing teaching skills through activities that are developmental, supportive, and aligned with teacher growth and success (Knapp & Feldman, 2012). Policy implementation offers opportunities to translate beliefs and actions into positive continuous improvement for an organization and teacher growth strategies within the context of accountability.

For further guidance on this case, please see the following:

American Civil Liberties Union. (2014, December). *Teaching kids, not stereotypes.* https://www.aclu.org/womens   -rights/teach-kids-not-stereotypes .

National Public Radio. (2014, December). *Debating single-sex classrooms.* On point with Tom Ashbrook. http://onpoint.wbur.org/2014/ 12/03/single-sex-classrooms-education-reform.

Sax, L. (2012, June). Know what's best for your child. *The New York Times*, opinion pages. http://www.nytimes.com/roomfordebate/2011/ 10   /17/single-sex-schools-separate-but-equal/know-whats-best-for-your-child.

U.S. Department of Education Office for Civil Rights. (2014, December). *Questions and answers on Title IX and single-sex elementary and secondary classes and extracurricular activities.* http://www2.ed.gov/ about/offices /list/ocr/docs/faqs-title-ix-single-sex-201412.pdf.

QUESTIONS FOR DISCUSSION

1. What type of power does Dr. Brock possess? What type of power does Mr. Lawrence have? How are curriculum decisions made at Roosevelt Elementary? What impact might this have on their implementation and outcomes?
2. How was vision developed in this case? What more could have been done?
3. Discuss the role of teamwork and collaboration in vision attainment.
4. Do you agree with Mr. Lawrence's philosophy of single-sex education? Mr. Lawrence argues that girls will be safer to voice their opinions when boys are absent. Is this a gender issue or a teaching issue?
5. What are the drawbacks of separating the sexes in this school?
6. As a new teacher who has altered his life to join this school community, should Mr. Chambers speak up? If he does, what should his

approach be? Do Mr. Chamber's values align with the school's values? Is this a good fit?

7. Although we do not know the background of Ms. Stanley, and her level of risk in broaching any questions as a new hire, should she speak up?
8. Is the curriculum strategy noted in this case representative of best practice? Why or why not?
9. Do the girls subjected to these curricular changes face more serious implications for their learning and social development than the boys? Why or why not? Justify your responses.
10. What would you do if you were the principal faced with the Third Grade Reading Guarantee? Is Dr. Brock making the best choices for her students? For her staff? Why or why not? Justify your responses with evidence.
11. Although this case details a predominantly white institution with predominantly white teachers, single-sex programming often occurs in urban environments with racially diverse populations. Why do you think this is the case? What are the implications of single-sex educational programming in urban environments with diverse student populations?
12. What should Mr. Chambers, Ms. Stanley, and Ms. Blankenship do collectively with their plan? What should their first steps be?
13. How would transgender students be impacted by single-sex education?
14. Ms. Blankenship is the only teacher of color at Roosevelt Elementary. What do you think her experiences are at this school? Why do you think her claims were ignored?
15. Discuss your perceptions of and experiences with "faddism" in education. What does Ms. Blankenship mean by this? Can you provide some examples?
16. Is this a case of discrimination? Justify your response.

NOTE

1. For a history of the "boy crisis" in education, see http://www.washingtonpost.com/wp-dyn/content/article/2006/04/07/AR2006040702025.html

REFERENCES

Asera, R. Johnson, J. F., & Ragland, M. A. (1999). *Urgency, responsibility, efficacy: Preliminary findings of a study of high-performing Texas school districts.* http://www.starcenter.org/services/main.htm#product.
Bennis, W., & Nanus, B. (2007). *Leaders. Strategies for Taking Charge.* New York, NY: Collins Business.

Boisot, M. (1995). *Information space: A framework of learning in organizations, institutions, and culture.* London, UK: Routledge.

Boyd, V. (1992). Creating a context for change: Issues about change. *SEDL, 2*(2).

Carter, R. T. (2000). *Addressing cultural issues in organizations: Beyond the corporate context.* Thousand Oaks, CA: Sage Publications, Inc.

Clark, D. L., Lotto, L. S., & Astuto, T. A. (1984). Effective schools and school improvement: A comparative analysis of two lines of inquiry. *Educational Administration Quarterly, 20*(3), 41–68.

Educational Leadership Constituent Council. (2011). Educational Leadership Program Standards. *National Policy Board for Educational Administration.* http://www.ncate.org/LinkClick.aspx?fileticket=zRZI73R0nOQ%3D&tabid=676.

Eliot, L. (2010a). *Pink brain, blue brain: How small differences grow into troublesome gaps—and what we can do about it.* New York, NY: Houghton Mifflin.

Eliot, L. (2010b). The myth of pink and blue brains. *Educational Leadership, 68*(3), 32–36.

Else-Quest, N. M., Hyde, J. S., & Linn, M. C. (2010). Cross-national patterns of gender differences in mathematics: A meta-analysis. *Psychological Bulletin, 136,* 103–27.

Frick, D. (2004). *Robert K. Greenleaf: A life of servant leadership.* San Francisco, CA: Berrett-Koehler Publishers, Inc.

Fullan, M. (1985). Change process and strategies at the local level. *Elementary School Journal, 85*(3), 391–421.

Fullan, M. G., & Miles, M. B. (1992). Getting reform right: What works and what doesn't. *Phi Delta Kappan, 73*(10), 744–52.

Gurian, M. (2010). *Boys and girls learn differently! A guide for teachers and parents.* San Francisco, CA: Jossey-Bass.

Hoff Sommers, C. (2013, October). What schools can do to help boys succeed. *Time.* http://ideas.time.com/2013/10/28/what-schools-can-do-to-help-boys-succeed/.

Kaufman, R., Herman, J., & Watters, K. (1996). *Educational planning: Strategic, tactical, operational.* Lancaster, PA: Technomic.

Knapp, M. S., & Feldman, S. B. (2012). Managing the intersection of internal and external accountability: Challenge for urban school leadership in the United States. *Journal of Educational Administration, 50*(5), 666–94.

Louis, K. S., & Kruse, S. D. (1995). *Professionalism and community: Perspectives on reforming urban schools.* Thousand Oaks, CA: Corwin.

Louis, K. S., Leithwood, K., Wahlstrom, K. L., & Anderson, S. E. (2010). *Investigating the links to improved student learning: Final report of research findings.* Learning from leadership Project. CAREI, University of Minnesota.

Maschke, K. (Ed.). (1997). *Gender and American law: Educational equity.* New York, NY: Routledge.

Nyberg, D. (1981). *Power over power.* Ithaca, NY: Cornell University Press.

Sax, L. (2006). *Why gender matters: What parents and teachers need to know about the emerging science of sex differences.* New York, NY: Harmony Publishers.

Sherwin, G. (2014, December). *Treating school kids differently based on sex = discrimination.* American Civil Liberties Union. https://www.aclu.org/blog/womens-rights/ treating-school-kids-differently -based-sex-discrimination.

Sherwin, G. (2015, August 14). *The 8 crazy stereotypes used in Wisconsin to justify single-sex classes and how they're boomeranging back on administrators.* ACLU. https://www.aclu.org/blog/speak-freely/8-crazy-stereotypes-used-wisconsin-justify-single-sex-classes-and-how-theyre.

Sergiovanni, T. (2001). *Leadership: What's in it for the schools?* London, UK: Routledge Falmer.

Spillane, J. P., & Thompson, C. L. (1997). Reconstructing conceptions of local capacity: The local education agency's capacity for ambitious instructional reform. *Educational Evaluation and Policy Analysis, 19*(2), 185–203.

U.S. Department of Education Office for Civil Rights. (2014, December). Questions and answers on Title IX and single-sex elementary and secondary classes and extracurricular activities.   http://www2.ed.gov/about/offices/list/ocr/docs/faqs-title-ix-single-sex-201412.pdf.

U.S. Department of Education, National Center for Education Statistics. (2005). *The Nation's Report Card long-term trend: Trends in average reading scores by gender*. Washington, DC.

Chapter Three

Teens will be Teens, or Sexual Harassment?

LGBTQ Students and Deliberate Indifference

INTRODUCTION

This case is based on the real case of Derek Henkle (2001) who was awarded $451,000 in damages because his school failed to protect him from harassment. But, unfortunately, Derek is not alone. Bullying and harassment in education greatly impacts lesbian, gay, bisexual, transgender, and queer (LGBTQ) youth.

In 2013, the Gay, Lesbian, & Straight Education Network published their National School Climate Survey and found that schools tend to be hostile places for LGBTQ students, the majority of whom experience sexual harassment and discrimination at school because they may not conform to traditional gender binaries. Consequently, many students who identify as LGBTQ avoid school altogether. Gender bias also impacts those students who may not identify as LGBTQ, but are perceived as such.

LGBTQ students who experience school-based discrimination and harassment have more negative academic outcomes and psychological struggles than their non-LGBTQ peers. Although the rates of school-based discrimination and harassment for LGBTQ students have improved over the years, the overall school climate remains hostile for many.

This case deals with Corey Austin's struggle to gain acceptance with peers. Corey was a tenth-grade student at George Washington High School in Benson, Colorado. An openly gay student, Corey could not find the support he needed with his peers so he joined an LBGTQ teen support group at his local community center. In this case, Corey experiences repeated unsolicited and aggressive behavior with the intention to cause harm and creates a real or perceived imbalance between the perpetrator and victim.

The disparity manifested by discriminatory and exclusionary disciplinary mechanisms inhibited Corey from receiving justice and were clearly demonstrated in the reactions, or lack thereof, of faculty and administrators. A discussion of approaches that can be implemented to reduce the bullying/violence that occurs in and around schools is encouraged.

THE CASE

While attending George Washington High School in rural Benson, Colorado, tenth-grade student Corey Austin struggled as a prime target of peer-based bullying. An openly gay student, Corey found the support he needed when he joined an LBGTQ teen support group at his local community center. Soon, his peers from school learned of his attendance at the support group meeting, as it was near Happy's, a local restaurant and teen hot spot for the George Washington High School "in-crowd."

The Tuesday night support group was the subject of the "in-crowd's" Tuesday night entertainment. Standing around their cars at 9:00 pm when the restaurant was closing, teens would taunt those they knew were attending the adjacent community center's support group for LGBTQ youth by shouting homophobic slurs or talking loudly within the earshot of their victims about their disdain for the gay community.

The Benson Police Department and school officials both felt Happy's was a hotbed for trouble. Police were often called to Happy's for fighting, noise control, and lewd behavior. However, no reports were ever filed for harassment, public disturbance, or hate speech. Often, police would simply instruct the rowdy crowds to disperse. Officers often found a group of teenagers teasing, shouting derogatory remarks, and harassing a victim or a group of victims, and at times this led to unwanted physical contact such as kicking, touching, and punching.

Police officers dismissed these incidents as typical teenage scuffles. Likewise, a significant number of adults in Benson did not view these behaviors as bullying. The underreaction of adults often left the victim(s) excluded, experiencing emotional distress with no immediate recourse, and subsequent heightened ostracism from peers, for which their peers experienced no consequences.

A recent transfer to George Washington High School, Corey had no idea that his desire for support would expose him to further torment. Although he attempted to shield his face against the torments with the hood of his sweatshirt, he heard his name called along with slurs such as "fag," "queer," and threats of violence. He just managed to shut the door of his car when a rock was thrown at his driver's window. There was no physical damage, but the threat of additional violence was palpable. Although Corey was terrified to attend school the next day, he decided not to tell his parents.

Corey had come out to his parents years before, and, although they were supportive, he did not want to cause them additional stress, as they had recently moved in an attempt to improve their financial situation. With a heavy heart and fear dripping through every pore, Corey entered George Washington High School on Wednesday morning. He arrived to find the word "fag" written on his locker in black marker. There were no teachers or administrators in the hallway to assist him.

When Corey opened his locker to retrieve his book for first period, he found a folded up piece of paper. Before he could open it, he was surrounded by a group of male students. Without time to think, the students lassoed him with a rope and threatened to drag him from their truck for "as long as it took."

In an instant, Corey found himself on the floor, rope still around him, gasping for breath. Everyone else was gone and the first period bell was ringing. The folded note was still in his hand. He struggled to release himself from his binds. When he managed to free himself, he opened the note. "DIE FAG" was written in large ominous black lettering.

Instead of walking in late to first period, Corey chose to report the Tuesday night incident as well as the graffiti, lasso, and note incidents to the assistant principal, Mr. Fletcher. Carrying the rope and what little dignity he had left in his hands, Corey revealed everything he had experienced in the last two days. Mr. Fletcher smiled, got up from his desk, and maneuvered around the small office to sit next to Corey in the only other chair.

"Corey," he began, "You have got to trust me on this one. I have been doing this a long time. This is what teenagers do. You will be fine. You need to stand up to bullies because you will face this your whole life and you will need to learn to deal with being different. There are always those folks who are not going to accept you because of who you are. Now. Take a couple deep breaths, splash some water on your face, and go back to class," Mr. Fletcher advised. "Next time, stand up to them. Sometimes people bring bullying on themselves. I am not saying that is what you did, but, unfortunately, sometimes kids will do what they think they can get away with. Do not allow them to get away with it." Corey took some deep breaths, splashed some cool water on his face, and returned to class. But the harassment did not stop, no matter if Corey attempted to project strength and confidence, or if he retreated.

Walking down the hallways, navigating his way to his classes was like a gauntlet of torment. It was as if everyone knew his story. He was a pariah. Corey felt he had no one to turn to at school. He felt hopeless.

Mr. Fletcher was kind, but not very helpful in Corey's estimation. As he was new to the school, Corey had not established a group of friends and had no one to support him. When Corey returned to the LBGTQ teen support group, he learned that none of the members attended his school. About half, seven students, attended private schools or schools in neighboring districts; the rest had once attended George Washington High School, but were now being homeschooled.

When Corey inquired as to why many students had left George Washington, one young woman spoke up. "It's the harassment. You think what happened to you is *something*? That's nothing compared to what happened to all of us. I'm not gonna say who, but I'm talking sexual assault. The school knows, but they hide it. The only way to get through it is to pretend that you are straight, but even then . . ."

Corey left the support group having made a few positive connections with other teens, but not feeling any more positive about school. However, after learning of the pattern of harassment faced by LGBTQ students at George Washington High School as indicated by the support group participants, Corey felt determined to persevere.

Corey returned to school in search of allies. But he found no friendly faces when experiencing harassment in the hallways or in class. On Monday of the following week, while students were to be reading silently in English class, a student threw a book and hit Corey in the head. This assault was followed by the comment, "Fags deserve worse." Corey looked at his teacher imploringly, but Mr. Knopschneider looked right through him and pretended he saw and heard nothing. Corey was shocked and hurt by what he perceived to be a culture of silence.

Desperate for a reprieve, Corey confided in his parents. Always supportive and sympathetic of their son's needs, they requested a transfer to the one of the other two district's high schools. The superintendent granted the request, but on the stipulation that Corey remain silent about his sexuality. The superintendent argued that Corey's sexuality was not appropriate for the district's conservative population and their stance of abstinence-only education. The condition of his transfer was that Corey "keep his sexuality private."

Corey entered John Adams High School with a positive attitude. However, upon his arrival, his principal met him in the hallway and escorted him to his first class, advising him that if he tried harder to fit in and stopped "flaunting his lifestyle," he would find more acceptance among his peers. Although Corey felt he was starting fresh at John Adams High School, the harassment continued.

He felt as if everyone—students, teachers, and administrators—was aware of what had happened at his previous school, and continued with the same patterns. He felt as if he were living in a déjà vu. Although the transfer, in his mind and in the minds of his parents, was a fresh start, this was not the reality for Corey. Instead, Corey felt he was being set up for failure. The harassment continued, as did the silence from faculty, staff, and administrators.

On his second day at John Adams High School, Corey walked into his math class to find a crude drawing of himself on the whiteboard at the back of the classroom, labeled with his full name, and a penis drawn near his mouth. Some students entering the classroom laughed and jeered at him before taking their seats. The teacher, who sat at her desk at the front of the room, the picture in her purview, waited until the bell rang, when all the students had taken their seats, to erase it. However, she said nothing about the drawing, and said nothing to the students who taunted Corey.

Corey heard various homophobic taunts, via whispers, throughout the remainder of the class, never sure who was delivering them. They seemed to come from all sides of the room like an orchestrated chorus. Humiliated, Corey looked at again at this teacher imploringly, as if to say, "please help me." The teacher refused to meet his gaze. Corey then put his head down on the desk and kept it there for the rest of the class period.

During that first week at John Adams High School, Corey also experienced an incident in the cafeteria. As Corey sat alone at a table eating his lunch, a large group of students sitting at an adjacent table began yelling homophobic slurs and throwing food at him. Corey immediately walked over to a teacher who was supervising the lunch to report the behavior.

"Mr. Mathis, can you please help me, or let me leave?"

"What seems to be the trouble, son?" Mr. Mathis replied.

"Did you not just see what happened?" Corey questioned. "You were standing right there."

The teacher held up his hand, refused to listen, and demanded that Corey return to his seat. Corey continued to plead that returning to that seat was not safe, but the teacher continued to repeat the directive, "You are continuing to argue with me when I have asked you to return to your seat."

At that point, Corey attempted to leave the cafeteria. The teacher then called a security guard over and asked him to escort Corey to the principal's office to be suspended for failure to comply. All of this was in earshot of the group of students who were originally taunting Corey at the adjacent table. As the security guard escorted Corey from the cafeteria by the arm, the students cheered.

When Corey returned to school after a three-day suspension, he was determined to make a difference in the harassment he experienced, even if school officials were unwilling to do the same. On his first day back, with the support of his parents, Corey filled out the necessary paperwork to start a student organization. His desire was to organize a Gay Straight Alliance within the school.

In order to file the paperwork for a new student organization, a staff sponsor is necessary. Corey was able to find one sympathetic teacher to sign on to the proposal. He was also able to garner support from several students. Corey then approached the assistant principal who was in charge of extracurricular activities. Dr. Hughes looked from Corey to the application, and then back again. "These things take time. I will look into it. Now go to class," he stated.

The final incident that Corey experienced at John Adams High School was in the school's computer lab. Upon entering the lab with his English class to conduct online research, Corey found all the screens were displaying the drawing of Corey that appeared on the whiteboard in his math class with a variety of homophobic slurs added.

Corey immediately ran from the lab and headed to the principal's office, demanding to call his parents. His parents left work and rushed to the school to conference with the administrative staff. After reiterating the pattern of harassment that Corey experienced, the administrative staff denied any knowledge of the incidents.

However, the administrative team assured Corey and his parents that they would protect Corey from all incidents of harassment, but that he needed to "stop throwing his sexuality in other students' faces" and to "cease trying to convert other students to his lifestyle."

Corey's parents were dismayed by the conference and decided to contact an attorney. The attorney advised the family to document Corey's harassment, with names, dates, and specific details. The attorney indicated that she would meet with the family to determine their best course of action after the account was compiled and she had time to review it.

A few days later, Corey approached Dr. Hughes again about the status of the Gay Straight Alliance application, but Dr. Hughes claimed never to have received it. Discouraged and despondent, Corey's parents pulled him from the school. Corey then transferred a third time to the third and final high school in the district. At this third high school, school officials failed to intervene when Corey was physically assaulted in the gym locker room.

Deterred by the cost of retaining their attorney, Corey's parents then met with central office administrators, the superintendent, and his team. The solution for the district was to remove Corey from his third school and to enroll him in an adult, continuing education program, although he was too young to take the GED.

Corey's parents, having completed a detailed history of Corey's harassment, as requested by the attorney they consulted, threatened to take Corey's story to the media if the district could not provide Corey with a safe educational environment.

After one month in the adult, continuing education program, Corey found an online article on LGBTQ students who successfully sued their school districts under Title IX for failing to protect them from sexual harassment. He also learned that in lieu of retaining an attorney, he could file a complaint with the Office of Civil Rights.

TEACHING NOTES

Passed in 1972, Title IX of the Educational Amendments prohibits sex discrimination in schools. Title IX also protects all students of all genders and sexual orientations from sexual harassment. Students in federally funded institutions, public and private schools, colleges, and universities have a right to an education free from discrimination on the basis of sex, including equitable access to academic programs, activities, athletics, admissions, recruitment, and scholarships, and freedom from harassment based upon sex, gender, gender identity and expression, and sexual orientation.

Title IX also protects students from discrimination in academic and nonacademic activities because of pregnancy, birth, miscarriage, and abortion, and protects faculty, staff, and whistleblowers from sexual harassment, sex discrimination, and retaliation.

Sexual harassment is any unwanted sexual behavior including sexual assault, verbal and/or written comments, requests for sexual favors, unwelcome sexual advances, spreading of sexual rumors, the questioning of one's sexuality/sexual orientation, gestures, pictures or images, and/or physical coercion. Sexual harassment can be direct or indirect.

Parents and students may sue school districts under Title IX if districts show deliberate indifference in addressing claims of sexual harassment. Schools are responsible for protecting students from sexual harassment, including peer harassment based on sexual orientation.

Title IX can be applied when students are harassed for their failure to conform to gender norms, or their complaints are ignored. Moreover, anti-LGBTQ behavior can be construed as sexual harassment where a perpetrator's actions involve sexual gestures or similar conduct, and school personnel can be held liable if they fail to respond under these circumstances.

An additional requirement of Title IX is that all schools receiving federal funds, including kindergarten to twelfth-grade schools, colleges, and universities, are required to hire and train, or appoint and train, Title IX Coordinators to oversee complaints of sex discrimination and sexual harassment (Martin, Kearl, & Murphy, 2013). Additionally, school districts are required to make the identity and contact information of the Title IX Coordinator(s) public and available to students and parents. At the time of this writing, most kindergarten to twelfth-grade school districts are not in full compliance with the coordinator requirements of Title IX.

The development of practical guidelines for effective interventions in cases such as Corey's are crucial to creating a guideline package to enhance school climate and improve school discipline (U.S. Department of Education, 2014). According to U.S. Secretary of Education Arne Duncan, "too many schools are still struggling to create the nurturing, positive, and safe environments that we know are needed to boost student achievement and success. . . . No student or adult should feel unsafe or unable to focus in school, yet this is too often a reality" (U.S. Department of Education, 2014, p. 7).

The following questions are to be used for group discussion. It is the intent of the authors to encourage open dialogue and reflective practice on this important topic. Readers are encouraged to consider the connections between poor policies and practices that are counterproductive and inadvertently lead to intolerance.

QUESTIONS FOR DISCUSSION

1. What are the issues in this case?
2. What should Corey and his family do?
3. There are two separate issues of social justice and equity in this case. Explain both and describe your position on both of them.
4. There are also legal and ethical issues implicit in this case. What are the district's and school's legal and ethical responsibilities in this case? Were they upheld?
5. Did the schools Corey attended violate Title IX? If so, how?
6. What were the schools' responsibilities to Corey? Does the treatment that Corey faced constitute "deliberate indifference"?
7. Is it ever acceptable for a school administrator to tell a student to "hide their sexuality"?
8. As an administrator, how would you have handled the situation?
9. Can schools deny student requests to start a Gay Straight Alliance? Explain your position.
10. How would you describe the leadership of the schools described in this case? What would you do differently?
11. Why are schools and districts out of compliance with the Title IX Coordinator requirement? What do they have to gain from not publicizing Title IX Coordinator information?
12. What steps can an administrator take to create a positive school culture that is accepting of students with different perspectives and orientations? In what ways should counselors, faculty, and staff be involved?

13. What role did the bystanders in this case play? How might the leadership in the school empower bystanders to act on the behalf of a student who is being harassed?
14. Does professionalism play a role in this case? How might teachers and administrators set an example with their own behavior? How might student behavior be monitored, particularly in the hallways?
15. What types of training would you recommend for faculty, staff, administration, students, and parents in this community?

ADDITIONAL ACTIVITIES

1. Investigate the following website: http://www.tolerance.org/lgbt-best-practices. Working with a small group, discuss the idea of tolerance and its place in a school curriculum. What teachable moments can you identify in this case? What might the teachers and administrators have done to engage students in difficult conversations?
2. Discuss the following questions: How can we cultivate respect for those whom we encounter? Can cultivating respect reduce discrimination and stereotypes? Create a plan to facilitate a healthy school culture in one of the schools mentioned in this case, paying particular attention to Title IX compliance and note any professional development that may be necessary for students, teachers, administrators, and parents.

ADDITIONAL RESOURCES

GSA Network. (n.d.). Dealing with hostility and opposition. https://www.gsanetwork.org/resources/building-your-gsa/dealing-hostility-opposition.
Frontline. (n.d.). *Assault on gay America: The life and death of Billy Gaither*. PBS. http://www.pbs.org/wgbh/pages/frontline/shows/assault/.
Frontline. (n.d.). *Interview with Derek Henkle*. PBS. http://www.pbs.org/wgbh/pages/frontline/shows/assault/interviews/henkle.html.

REFERENCES

American Association of University Women. (2004). *Harassment-free hallways: How to stop sexual harassment in schools, a guide for students, parents, and schools*. Washington, DC: American Association of University Women. http://history.aauw.org/files/2013/01/harassment_free.pdf.
Benson, K. A. (1984). Comment on Crocker's An analysis of university definitions of sexual harassment. *Signs: Women, Culture, & Society, 9*(3), 516–19.
Espelage, D. L., Astor, R. A., Cornell, D., Lester, J., Mayer, M. J., Meyer, E. J., Poteat, V. P., & Tynes, B. (2013, April). Prevention of bullying in schools, colleges, and universities: Research report and recommendations. The American Educational Research Association. http://www.aera.net/Portals/38/docs/News%20Release/

Prevention%20of%20Bullying%20in%20Schools,%20Colleges%20and%20Universities.pdf.

Hill, C., & Kearl, H. (2011). *Crossing the line: Sexual harassment at school.* Washington, DC: American Association of University Women. http://www.aauw.org/files/2013/02/Crossing-the-Line-Sexual-Harassment-at-School.pdf.

Klein, S. (Ed.). *Handbook for achieving gender equity through education* (2nd ed.). Hillsdale, NJ: Erlbaum Publishers.

Kosciw, J. G., Greytak, E. A., Palmer, N. A., & Boesen, M. J. (2013). *The 2013 national school climate survey: The experiences of lesbian, gay, bisexual and transgender youth in our nation's schools.* New York: Gay, Lesbian, & Straight Education Network.

MacKinnon, C. A. (1979). *Sexual harassment of working women: A case of sex discrimination.* New Haven: Yale University Press.

Martin, J., Kearl, H., & Murphy, W. J. (2013). Bullying and harassment in schools: Analysis of legislation and policy. In M. A. Paludi (Ed.), *Women and management: Global issues and promising solutions. Volume 2: Signs of solutions* (pp. 29–51). Santa Barbara, CA: Praeger.

Meyer, E. J. (2009). *Gender, bullying, and harassment: Strategies to end sexism and homophobia in schools.* New York, NY: Teachers College Press.

Paludi, M. A. (1997). Sexual harassment in schools. In W. O'Donohue (Ed.), *Sexual harassment: Theory, research, and treatment* (pp. 225–49). Boston: Allyn and Bacon.

Sadowski, M. (2001). Sexual minority students benefit from school-based support—where it exists. *Harvard Education Letter, 17*(5), 1–5.

Stein, N. (1999b). *Classrooms and courtrooms: Facing sexual harassment in K-12 schools.* New York, NY: Teachers College Press.

Teaching Tolerance: A Project of the Southern Poverty Law Center. (2013). Best practices: Creating an LGBT-inclusive school climate. http://www.tolerance.org/lgbt-best-practices.

U.S. Department of Education. (2014). *Guiding principles: A resource guide for improving school climate and discipline* [Educational standards]. http://www2.ed.gov/policy/gen/guid/school-discipline/guiding-principles.pdf.

Chapter Four

Socio-economic Status and Student Opportunity

A Case of Disrespect or Teenage Rebellion?

INTRODUCTION

Brown v Board of Education (1954) was the U.S. Supreme Court case declaring separate public schools for black and white students unconstitutional, overturning *Plessy v Ferguson* (1896), which upheld state-sponsored segregation in public education. The Brown decision declared *de jure* racial segregation a violation of the Equal Protection Clause of the Fourteenth Amendment.

A major factor in the Brown case was the Clarks' "doll experiments" of the 1940s, illustrating how children were impacted by segregation. Kenneth and Mamie Clark, psychologists at Columbia University, presented participant children with two identical dolls, but for skin and hair color: one doll had brown skin and black hair, the other, white skin and blonde hair.

The children were then asked which doll they preferred and various other questions such as which one looks "bad" and which has the "nicer color." The children showed an overall preference for the white doll, which illustrated internalized racism among Black children. Such feelings of self-hatred were more pronounced in children who attended segregated schools (American Psychological Association, 2014).

As Kenneth Clark stated, "The Negro child accepts as early as six, seven, or eight the negative stereotypes about his own group. . . . These children . . . like other human beings who are subjected to an obviously inferior status in the society in which they live, have been definitely harmed in the development of their personalities" (Clark, as cited in Beggs, 1995, n. p.). Such harm, of which Clark speaks, still impacts our Black and Brown children in U.S. schools. To wit, new data from the U.S. Department of Education's Office for Civil Rights (2014) illustrate how racism and structural inequalities impact schools today.

Some of the most shocking findings from these data include the following: although Black students account for only 18 percent of U.S. pre-kindergarten enrollment, they account for 48 percent of *preschoolers* [our emphasis] with multiple suspensions; Black students are expelled three times more than their white counterparts; Black and Latina/o students account for 40 percent of enrollment at schools offering gifted programs, but only 26 percent of students in said programs; Black, Latina/o students, and Native American students attend schools with higher percentages of first-year teachers (3 to 4 percent) than their white counterparts (1 percent); and Black students are more than three times as likely to attend schools where less than 60 percent of teachers meet all state requirements for certification and licensure.

The above findings have great implications for our kindergarten to twelfth-grade schools, for higher education, and for society in general. The issue of financial and resource equity in education continues to be a crucial issue. Can the heart of our nation be judged by the allocation of their resources? Tellingly, more resources are allocated to incarceration than to education.

Despite the fact that the United States is one of the wealthiest nations, the United States comprises 5 percent of the world's population and 25 percent of the world's inmates (Darling-Hammond, 2013). As Kozol (2005) argues, the discrepancy in funding for public schools in the United States disproportionately impacts the poor and people of color, leading to an intractable opportunity gap. The glaring question remains: how far are we from *Brown*?

Although *Brown* was decided over fifty years ago, we are not metaphorically far from the above-mentioned feelings of students of color illustrated by the Clarks' experiments, trapped in segregated schools and reduced to feelings of inferiority. This issue of equitable school funding is not only relevant to those students attending these schools, but to society in general. We must do better to equitably educate our children.

This is a complex case involving "intersectionality." Intersectionality as a theoretical construct functions to describe the experience of individuals possessing interlocking oppressions and/or multiple minority statuses and a depiction of the lived experience of individuals who possess identities that may or may not conflict in their political orientations. This case intentionally focuses explicitly on socio-economic status, and implicitly on race. This intentionality highlights the "colorblindness" of the staff working at the school described in this case.

This case alludes to the racial tensions surrounding access to public pools in American history. Even today, we feel the implications of both legalized and socially imposed segregation in this area. To wit, approximately 58 percent of African American children do not know how to swim, which is double the rate of white children (Wiltse, 2007). Also, African Americans are three times more likely to be victims of drowning (National Public Radio, 2008).

This case examines the experiences of Dr. Marcia Moore, administrator of the Cambridge Summer Sports Camp (CSSC) Program, and Mr. Jim Grier, physical education teacher, born and raised in the community. Their personal experiences with race and class converge after a controversial incident, which may or may not be classified as a student discipline infraction.

THE CASE

A school district is dependent on the support, resources, and involvement of a community and its members. In addition to collaborative community support, population demographics and history, including socio-economic factors and population growth, greatly impact the financial stability and growth of the school district. Likewise, the overall performance and success of the school district may have a direct impact on the growth and property values of a community (Chiodo, Hernandez-Murillo, & Owyang, 2010).

The economy and population of Cambridge, Pennsylvania, has declined steadily since the closing of the steel mills in the late 1970s. The population decreased from 167,000 people in 1960 to 65,000 by 2015. The city, which had once relied heavily on manufacturing jobs, is now in a state of economic decline contributing to a lack of educational advancement, lower salaries, and high unemployment.

The Cambridge City School District has an enrollment of approximately 5,100 students with 20 percent of the population receiving services for students with disabilities. This program serves 98 percent economically disadvantaged students of which 85 percent African American and 15 percent White. Although many graduates of the Cambridge School District pursue college degrees, few return to the area due to the shortage of career opportunities in the city and county. Only 62 percent of the overall population has earned a high school diploma. In addition, 25 percent of Cambridge residents currently hold a Bachelor's degree, while only 4 percent have earned a graduate degree.

The median combined household income in 2015 was $24,500, well below the state average of $47,000 per household. The Department of Job and Family Services reports that 18 percent of all residents throughout the county currently live below the federal poverty level. In comparison, 36.4 percent of the adults and 63.3 percent of the children currently residing in Cambridge are currently living below poverty level, with many families receiving cash and food assistance, child care subsidies, access to basic medical and dental care, as well as access to early learning opportunities for children through the Head Start Program.

Research clearly shows a relationship between school level poverty and student academic performance. As the level of poverty increases in a school, student performance declines (Betts, Rueben, & Danenberg, 2000; Coleman, 1966; Datcher, 1982; Grissmer, Flanagan, Kawata, & Williamson, 2000).

Case Background: The Cambridge City School District

The percentage of students classified as economically disadvantaged has steadily increased over the past twenty years. The 2014-2015 Cambridge School District Report Card stated that 98 percent of the five thousand students enrolled in the district are classified as economically disadvantaged. The district is currently ranked last of the school districts in the state.

Although evidence does not suggest that district performance is contributing to population and economic decline within the City of Cambridge, the impact of population demographics and socio-economic factors are evident in the school district. Enrollment numbers have declined substantially over the years, and, as property values have declined, lower property tax revenue has had a deleterious effect on the district budget.

The Cambridge City School District has been ill equipped to support the needs of the growing population of economically challenged students attending their schools. No training was provided for teachers to address the changing needs of students, many of whom come to school hungry and below state expectations for their grade level. Families in this area tend to be transient because jobs and resources are scarce.

Parents typically must work two or three jobs in order to make ends meet. This has great implications for the children currently residing in this area. Because parents are often away from the home working, older siblings are responsible for feeding and tending to the homework needs of their younger siblings—often areas beyond their expertise. In areas of economic insecurity, gangs tend to flourish as recently evidenced by the explosion of gang activity in Cambridge.

The Cambridge City School District is aware of the societal economic issues that families residing in their district experience. Although they have little control over these issues, the superintendent, Dr. Livingston, wrote a five-year federal grant in order to assist parents in the district. Her plan was to expand the district's summer school program, from a credit and retention recovery program, to a summer enrichment program for all students in the district so that parents could focus on work and cease to worry about their children falling prey to gang influences within their neighborhoods.

Case Narrative: The Cambridge Summer Sports Camp

In an effort to provide a summer enrichment program to an underserved population, the Cambridge City School District gained federal funding through Title II to support the Cambridge Summer Sports Camp (CSSC) focusing on sports and physical activity. Although many of the students in the district were in need of literacy and math skills, the majority testing well below grade level, the superintendent determined that a more pressing need was to repair the negative perceptions the community held of the schools. Dr. Livingston felt that easing the pressures of childcare might help repair the multiple decade–long divide between the school and the community.

Dr. Livingston was unaware of the cause of this divide. In fact, most teachers and administrators were unaware that such a divide and distrust among parents even existed. The historical knowledge of the community among school district employees was not well known; this was exacerbated by the high rate of teacher turnover that is common in urban areas.

Despite these facts, Dr. Livingston was confident that the camp could do much to bridge these divides. She determined that this measure would do more for the community than she could do by talking to district employees about historic strife. In her experience, she had found that educators have difficulty in dealing with long-range systemic problems.

Instead, teachers are accustomed to "quick fix" and top-down initiatives. Likewise, she surmised that her parents were too busy to become involved and were likely not well informed about what their children needed in order to be successful in school. Moreover, the feds had approved her initiative and funded it well. She was confident that the summer program would be successful.

The Cambridge Summer Sports Camp

The new initiative, the CSSC, consisted of a summer-long series of active sports training camps. The day camps provide specific sports training in baseball, basketball, inline hockey, lacrosse, soccer, softball, tennis, and volleyball. All children, grades three through ten, enrolled in Cambridge City Schools and residing in a low-income household were eligible, but enrollment was limited based on funding.

Campers arrived every morning at 8:30 am and left at 5:00 pm. Activities included warm ups/stretching, lessons, drills, small group instruction, breakfast and lunch, free time, scrimmaging, and a break period where children could watch movies or rest. Supplemental classroom activities such as drug and alcohol awareness, team building, and sex education for older students were also scheduled. For six weeks each summer, students were provided free breakfast and lunch through the U.S. Department of Agriculture summer food service program. The camp was provided to students at no cost with funding from the federal grant.

The First Year

In the first year, the CSSC quickly grew in popularity. Working parents were anxious for a safe place for their children to go in the summer, away from the growing negative influences of the neighborhood; this program fulfilled that need. At the close of the first year, the program administrators were thrilled with the success of the CSSC. Attendance was high and the children seemingly enjoyed the activities. Dr. Livingston and program directors felt that the parents were thankful for CSSC as a safe haven from the gang activity that ruled the neighborhoods because they diligently ensured their children's attendance.

However, in the first year, program enrollment only reached 158 with a target of 200. Reasons for the underenrollment were investigated by Dr. Livingston, who determined that the target was not reached because of student transportation. Because of budget cuts, bussing had been drastically reduced during the school year and no bussing was available for summer programs. During the first year, parents and guardians were responsible for getting their children to and from camp.

The program administrator, Dr. Marcia Moore, felt strongly about finding a way to ease the burden of transportation for parents. Additionally, Dr. Livingston communicated to Dr. Moore that the goal for year two was three hundred students. Because of this charge, Dr. Moore decided to use the public transportation system to get students to and from the program. Dr. Livingston thoroughly endorsed this idea, as she believed this would alleviate pressure from the parents and serve to further ingratiate the parents to the school district.

The Second Year

Once accepted into the program for the second year, parents received a letter welcoming them. The welcome letter included a sample daily schedule, breakfast and lunch menus, and an explanation of the bus transportation system.

Although some parents still relied on their own personal transportation both to and from the camp in year two, the majority of parents sent their children to camp through the public transportation system. Parents explained to their children which bus stop to exit for the summer program, but many did not tell their child what exit to take to get back home. As the staff loaded the busses at the end of the first day, students got on not knowing when to get off, and many missed their exits.

As Dr. Moore turned to leave at the end of her first day, she heard the phone ring. One parent after another called to find out where their child was. One child who did not know where to get off stayed on the bus and ended up at the bus station. Immediately, Dr. Moore called her office staff back in to help field calls. She also contacted the public transportation bus system. Dr. Moore had no experience riding public transportation; in fact, Dr. Moore's inexperience of the public transportation system, and that of her staff, created this problem.

Dr. Moore felt that the creation of a master schedule would alleviate all future transportation issues. That night she and her office secretary mapped bus routes and student stops. Dr. Moore had assumed that when the students came to school on the bus that they would know how to get home. Despite the master schedule, another glitch occurred.

The bus pass system involved a summer camp staff member escorting the students to the bus stop where they would hand each student a bus pass to get home and another pass to return the next day. The box of bus passes were budgeted to last 65 percent of students enrolled in the camp thirty days. Because bus duty rotated among staff members, the passes were kept in the main office where they were readily accessible to staff. A few weeks into the program, bus passes were disappearing. There were not enough passes to make it to the end of the program, and additional funds would be needed to secure the necessary bus passes. After some investigation, Dr. Moore determined that the shortage in bus passes was caused by student theft. However, no student was found to be the culprit of said theft.

As the second year of the program closed, Dr. Moore held a staff meeting to discuss the outcomes of the program and improvements that were needed for the next year. Other than the missing bus passes, the second year had ended with great success. Student enrollment was at full capacity, children and parents were happy, and funding was continued for the following year.

However, staff member Jim Grier expressed his concern over the use of bus passes. Jim was a beloved physical education teacher in the district. The students respected Mr. Grier. He was known to be fair and to genuinely care about the students. Also, he saw the benefits the CSSC offered his students: a safe place to be in the summer months away from gangs and street life, much needed meals (breakfast and lunch), and good role models.

Mr. Grier grew up in the neighborhood and still resided in the area. He was well aware of the gang violence to which his students were subject, and he felt the system of using bus passes for students to get to and from camp was not well thought out and wrought with potential disaster. He felt the students were too young to be riding public transportation alone.

The Third Year

In the third year of the program, Dr. Moore devised an innovative idea for systematizing the bus passes. The system would include a lanyard with a permanent bus pass for each student requiring transportation to and from CSSC, including the beginning and ending date of the program, times of pre-paid transportation (arrival and departure from CSSC), and each student's name and photo.

On the first day of camp, the public transportation system, Western Reserve Transit Authority, better known as WRTA, came to school and took students' pictures. Bus passes were laminated and put on lanyards for the students. With 320 enrolled in the program, the use of bus passes had risen to 90 percent of participants.

At first, things ran smoothly with students arriving to school and going home by bus on time and without difficulty. But two weeks into the summer program on a Wednesday morning, only 180 students showed up for school. Mr. Grier, the only African American employee in the summer program, was on bus duty that morning and he was the first to report that most of the students who rode the buses did not show up for camp. His concern for the students was evident as he pressed Dr. Moore to call WRTA.

Unalarmed, Dr. Moore knew that student attendance varied because it was summer and families' schedules were subject to change. But as the attendance sheets came into the office, her concern grew. The attendance sheets showed that the younger students who rode the bus were in school; it was the older students who were absent.

Dr. Moore thought this was peculiar that only the older students were not at school. As one of the younger students, Kesha, entered the office, Dr. Moore took the opportunity to ask where her older brother was. Kesha disclosed, "They all went to the mall today." Dr. Moore surmised that as students became accustomed to using the bus passes, they figured out they could ride the public buses anywhere, and they wanted to go to the mall.

Knowing that Mr. Grier was well acquainted with the students, Dr. Moore called him into the office to tell him what she had discovered. Mr. Grier quickly offered to go to the mall to locate the students. Dr. Moore returned to her office to inform parents of the situation. As Mr. Grier walked through the mall, he encountered the missing students and informed them that they were not supposed to use their bus passes to travel anywhere other than school and back home. He escorted many to the bus stop and waited for the appropriate bus to arrive. He drove the remaining students home in his own car.

Dr. Moore and her secretary worked all afternoon and late into the evening calling parents and guardians to explain what had happened. Most of the parents did not know that the students had used the bus passes to go to the mall. The students had arrived at their homes at their normal time to avoid getting in trouble with their parents. While most parents were upset about the situation, some were not at all troubled. As one parent remarked, "Well you gave them a pass. It was just something that kids know how to do—ride the bus. What did you expect? They are teenagers."

Dr. Moore was upset with her students, their parents, and the entire situation. She was livid at the ungratefulness of the students, who were provided with an amazing opportunity that, she believed, would ultimately help them with their academic progress, keep them out of trouble, and provide unique summer programming that would benefit their health. She expressed these sentiments to Mr. Grier when he came to her office to meet with her the next morning. She had called upon him to express her outrage.

Mr. Grier was not shy about expressing his concerns. "With all due respect, Dr. Moore, you have no idea what it is like to live in this community. I grew up here. Just give me a few moments to tell you a story." Mr. Grier paused and looked at Dr. Moore. She nodded.

"When I was a little kid, this community was more integrated. I mean, don't get me wrong. There were white neighborhoods and black neighborhoods. Although this is not the south, Jim Crow lived here. We had a public pool, but it was for 'whites only.' Everyone knew this. After the *Brown* decision, parents started sending their children to the pool. But instead of welcoming us, they drained it.

This is the legacy in which we live. Now, I was a little too young to experience that myself, but my older brothers and sisters lived that reality. Can you imagine what that does to a person? Knowing that you are undervalued so much that community members would rather take the opportunity for swimming away from everyone, rather than have black children in the pool?"

"I am sorry this happened, Mr. Grier," Dr. Moore replied, "but I am not sure I see the connection."

"I said that this might take a while, Dr. Moore." Mr. Grier smiled. "You see, kids know immediately whether they are valued by the adults around them. I mean, they might not be able to articulate it, but they understand if they are valued as human beings, or if they are looked down upon by the adults who are in authority over them. The older kids, they may have gotten that message. And, despite your best intentions, they are not going to respect you if you do not respect them.

Again, the kids may not be able to articulate this, surely not if *you* asked them, but even if *I* did. But I suspect that this action is an assertion of their autonomy, of their personhood."

"I totally understand what you are saying, Mr. Grier, and I respect it. But I take issue with the fact that any adult working in this program has communicated any notion that we do not value the students," Dr. Moore implied, feeling her pulse rise.

"Again, with all due respect," Mr. Grier began tentatively, "I disagree. Think about it this way. Yes, these students, many come from poverty. Their parents work multiple jobs, with crazy unstable hours, and so they may not be able to come into the school, help their children with homework, and some of these teachers take that to mean that the parents do not care about their kids. But this perception comes from their own lives, from their own recollections of what *their* childhoods were like, or from their own parenting styles.

Do the teachers here ever try to get to know the lived experiences of our kids? Also, the curriculum, particularly in the early grades—it is highly scripted. The literacy program? *Success for All*? I call it 'Success for None.' This is nothing less than a watered down curriculum presuming that our kids are stupid and incapable of critical thought. The reading materials have nothing to do with their home lives, cultures, languages, or community. Can you say that you would endorse such a curriculum for your own children?"

Dr. Moore was torn between throwing Mr. Grier out of her office and listening. Although she felt her face flush and perspiration flow seemingly out of each and every pore of her body, she decided to pause. She nodded. "I am listening."

"I know I am just a gym teacher. This is not a job that carries much prestige, but I have never cared about that. All I ever wanted to do was to live and work in the community that I love—the community I grew up in, the community that made me who I am. But I know these kids. And, I am not going to say that I am not mad as hell at them, because I am. But I want to tell you, that I *understand*. I understand why they did what they did. When I was putting them on their buses to return home yesterday, I pulled Jamal to the side. Do you know Jamal?"

Dr. Moore shook her head to indicate that she did not, feeling the guilt rise within her for not knowing one of her students.

Mr. Grier nodded. "I asked Jamal what they were thinking. Whose idea this was. And do you know what he said to me?"

Dr. Moore closed her eyes and shook her head again, her anger subsiding.

"He said it was the first time in his life that he felt free. He felt free to be able to go and hang out with his friends at the mall—something that teenagers in the suburbs have the opportunity to do all the time. Am I right?"

"You are not incorrect." Dr. Moore suddenly realized that there were many problems within her school that she was not privy to. She wondered just how foolish she looked to the community.

"Again, Dr. Moore, I am not telling you that I am not upset with these kids. In fact, I am very upset. But, given the opportunity for free travel, as a kid, I am not sure I would not have done the same. What I am saying is that this issue is not just about kids breaking rules. It is about so much more. And let's talk about lacrosse. I mean, who, outside of prep schools and liberal arts colleges, even knows what the heck that is? And what suburban kid has to be shuttled to school every day over the summer, not having any choice in what to do on any given day?"

Although Dr. Moore was surprised that the students in the program would use their knowledge of the public transportation system, knowledge that she did not possess, to serve their own needs, upon reflection, she wondered, *if given the opportunity in my own teenage rebellion phase: would I have done the same?* Dr. Moore then thought of how many times she had disobeyed her own parents. However, the difference here was that her students were supported by a federal grant.

Dr. Moore felt she needed to question everything. Was the program what the students needed? Why had the district not consulted the community, the parents, in how to best address the needs of their student population? Had she been viewing her students from a deficit mindset as Mr. Grier implied? Would such a paternalistic program ever fly in the suburbs? Why did educators deem parents living in poverty to be uninvolved or uncaring about their children's educations? All of these questions flew through her mind as she sat across from Mr. Grier who was now silent, waiting for her to speak.

Dr. Moore sighed. "Mr. Grier. I thank you for your candor. I really do. You have given me so much to think about, and I have a lot of thinking yet to do. But, let me ask you: Where do you see us going from here?"

"Before I get to that, I have one more question for you, Dr. Moore. I do not necessarily want you to answer it, but I ask you to think about it. Why did you ask me to come and speak to you about this issue? Are you speaking with all of the teachers?"

Dr. Moore thought for a moment. But she knew the answer. She did not even think about asking any of the other teachers, all of whom were white, to speak to her. She had only asked to speak with Mr. Grier.

QUESTIONS FOR DISCUSSION

1. What would you do if you were Dr. Moore? What is the future of this summer program? How would you change it?
2. Should Dr. Moore discipline the students involved in the bus incident? Explain your answer.
3. Explain the bravery of Mr. Grier in speaking candidly to Dr. Moore. What risks did he take in doing so?
4. Would such a summer program ever impact middle-class students?
5. Why did Dr. Moore ask only Mr. Grier to speak to her about the issue at hand? Was she implicitly asking him to speak for his community? His race?

6. Why did Dr. Livingston not speak to the community about their needs? As an educational leader, what would you do differently?
7. What do you think of the historical divide between the school and community? What would you do differently as an educational leader to investigate the root of the problem?

ADDITIONAL ACTIVITIES

1. Research the history on public pool segregation. What are the historical and lasting impacts on communities in light of this history?
2. How is this case a case involving "intersectionality"? Intersectionality as a theoretical construct functions to describe the experience of individuals possessing interlocking oppressions and/or multiple minority statuses and a depiction of the lived experience of individuals who possess identities that may or may not conflict in their political orientations. The concept presupposes that a single lens is inadequate in communicating the various and diverse oppressions that many individuals face. In small groups, discuss this concept and how it applies to this case.
3. In small groups, discuss student needs in high poverty schools. How can educators develop personal skills for working with children in poverty? Make a list of core competencies that are needed to work with students in poverty. Evaluate your skills. Make a check next to each core competency to indicate if you have the skill.

REFERENCES

American Psychological Association. (2014). *Featured psychologists: Mamie Phipps Clark, Ph.D. and Kenneth Clark, Ph.D.* http://www.apa.org/pi/oema/resources/ethnicity-health/psychologists/clark.aspx.
Betts, J., Rueben, K., & Danenberg, K. (2000). *Equal resources, equal outcomes? The distribution of school resources and student achievement in California.* San Francisco, CA: Public Policy institute of California.
Chiodo, A. J., Hernandez-Murillo, R., & Owyang, M. T. (2010). Nonlinear effects of school quality on house prices. *Federal Reserve Bank of St. Louis Review, 92*(3), 185–204.
Coleman, J. S. (1966) *Equality of education opportunity study.* Washington, DC: U.S. Department of Health, Education, and Welfare, Office of Education/National Center for Education Statistics.
Datcher, L. (1982). Effects of community and family background on achievement. *Review of Economics and Statistics, 64,* 32–41.
Grissmer, D., Flanagan, A., Kawata, J. & Williamson, S. (2000). *Improving student achievement: What state NAEP test scores tell us.* Santa Monica, CA: RAND.
Darling-Hammond. L. (2013). Diversity, equity, and education in a globalized world. *Kappa Delta Pi Record, 49*(3), 113–15.
Kozol, J. (2005). *The shame of the nation: The restoration of apartheid schooling in America.* New York, NY: Random House.

National Public Radio. (2008). *Racial history of American swimming pools.* http://www.npr. org/templates/story/story.php?storyId=90213675.

U.S. Department of Education Office for Civil Rights. (2014, March). *Civil rights data collection, data snapshot: School discipline.* http://www2.ed.gov/about/offices/list/ocr/docs/crdc-discipline-snapshot.pdf.

Wiltse, J. (2007). *Contested waters: A social history of swimming pools in America.* Chapel Hill, NC: The University of North Carolina Press.

Chapter Five

Islamophobia in Suburbia

Religious Freedom or Intolerance?

INTRODUCTION

Although the United States purports to be a nation of individuals free to express their religious liberty, our history is rife with the banning and burning of books, religious and otherwise. This case asks the reader to examine whether public school teachers should be free to engage students in the discussion of various religious traditions. This case also hints at the aspect of the customer service model, which has found its way into education. An implicit question raised in this case is: is education a business or a service?

This case also addresses the phenomenon of Islamophobia, which is an illogical fear, hatred, and/or hostility of/toward Islamic people, and includes negative stereotypes that result in bias, discrimination, and/or marginalization and exclusion of Muslims from all aspects of public life. The rise of Islamophobia can be directly tied to the terrorist attacks of September 11, 2001.

Although public schools are open to all members of the public, regardless of their faith, the issue of the proper role of religion in public schools continues to be a subject of great controversy. School districts must set forth clear policies regarding religion in the public schools that satisfy both the letter and the spirit of the First Amendment. This case is ultimately about the role of religion in the public school curriculum.

THE CASE

In this land of equal liberty it is our boast, that a man's religious tenets will not forfeit the protection of the Laws, nor deprive him of the right of attaining and holding the highest Offices that are known in the United States.
–George Washington, 1793

Tim Wilkinson teaches history at Spring Hills High School in Henderson, West Virginia. He has been a teacher at Spring Hills for seventeen years. Early in his career, Mr. Wilkinson developed an elective class in World Studies. The elective, which has been taught for fifteen years, includes a unit on world religions covering five traditions: Christianity, Judaism, Buddhism, Hinduism, and Islam. In past years, students visited a Christian church, a synagogue, a Hindu temple, and a mosque. Although Mr. Wilkinson desired for his students to visit a Buddhist place of worship, there was not one in the area.

Mr. Wilkinson strongly believes that despite America being such a religiously diverse nation, religious literacy is lacking, particularly in this part of his region of the country where diversity in general is sparse. To wit, in a 2005 study conducted for the Bible Literacy Project, only 10 percent of American teenagers could even name the five world religions covered in the world religions unit at Spring Hills High School (Wachlin & Johnson, 2005).

Mr. Wilkinson argues that religious literacy is necessary for a healthy democratic and pluralistic society. Religion is not a discrete and ahistorical phenomenon; instead, it is embedded in the very fabric of human history and culture. Without some understanding of the world's religious traditions, so argues Mr. Wilkinson, students will be ill equipped to fully comprehend literature, history, art, or even government and politics.

Examining other religious traditions and conflict narratives or divergences from one's own moral code can allow students to cultivate moral agency by affecting their perspectives and self-sanctions (Bandura, Caprara, Barbaranelli, Pastorelli, & Regalia, 2001).

Moral agency is the capacity to understand, practice, and engage in actions and behaviors which are considered right to an individual's moral system (Bandura, Caprara, Barbaranelli, Pastorelli, & Regalia, 2001; Caprara, Tisak, Alessandri, Fontaine, Fida, & Paciello, 2014). Adherence to a moral code prevents individuals from behaving immorally and helps to maintain social order (Bandura, Caprara, Barbaranelli, Pastorelli, & Regalia, 2001).

Empowering students to ask "big questions" facilitates moral engagement by sharing and organizing information, making meaning, and understanding different perspectives (Baumeister, Zhang, & Vohs, 2004). One Spring Hills' alumnus remarked that the World Studies class "was really the one and only class that allowed for such an open dialogue of faith and religion."

On Friday, November 1, Mr. Wilkinson received a phone message in his mailbox stating that a parent, Joe Richards and father to Mr. Wilkinson's tenth-grade student Ashley, would not permit his child to visit a mosque and desired that she be removed from his course. Mr. Wilkinson had distributed permission slips for this particular field trip on Monday of the same week.

Mr. Wilkinson had nothing but positive experiences with Ashley prior to this incident. In fact, she had already visited a Jewish temple and an African Methodist Episcopal Church previously that semester.

Perplexed, Mr. Wilkinson made a call to the home. He was sure that there was some mistake. Mr. Wilkinson planned what to say as he heard the phone ring. Mrs. Richards answered the phone.

Mr. Wilkinson identified himself and explained the message that he had received and asked if he could explain the situation. "Thank you Mr. Wilkinson," Mrs. Richards stated curtly, "but we have no desire to speak with you on this matter or any other. Besides, my husband is not here to tell you this himself, but if he were, I am confident that he would not be as kind as I. Please do not call again." And with that, the call ended.

Mr. Wilkinson felt as if he had just been slapped in the face. As it was the beginning of his planning period, he left his classroom and walked down the hallway to the counseling office. He thought that speaking to Ashley's counselor, Ms. Davis, would provide some insight into the family and how he could better handle this situation.

Seeing her door open, he entered Ms. Davis's office and asked if he could shut the door. "This must be serious," Ms. Davis replied, and nodded. Mr. Wilkinson shut the door and sat down in the chair adjacent to her desk. "Would you like some coffee?"

"No," Mr. Wilkinson replied, "thank you, but I think that would make me more tense than I already am. I cannot believe what just happened. Are you familiar with the family of Ashley Richards?"

Ms. Davis chuckled wryly, "They called you too, huh?" she asked. Mr. Wilkinson nodded. "Proceed with extreme caution here. This situation has the potential of being very contentious. Mr. Richards called me at 7:00 am demanding that Ashley be pulled from your course immediately. Apparently he had no idea that she was even in the course, or that she had been on any other field trips with you."

Mr. Wilkinson was taken aback. "But she had signed permission slips for both of those trips."

"Apparently there is going to be an investigation," Ms. Davis began. "Mr. Richards is claiming that her mother would not have signed those permission slips, and had he known that she was in this course he would have pulled her months ago. He is claiming educational fraud and is demanding that she be given a passing grade in your class, but that she will no longer attend, do any readings, or any work assigned by you. He desires that she finish the rest of the semester in another course. He is claiming that you are promoting Islamic tolerance."

"I am at a loss for words," Mr. Wilkinson replied.

"I am not sure how successful this will be, but the only thing to do might be to arrange a meeting," Ms. Davis suggested.

Mr. Wilkinson thought it best, based upon his knowledge of Mr. Richards's anger, that they hold the conference in the principal's office, with the principal present. After leaving Ms. Davis's office, Mr. Wilkinson immediately went to the office of the principal, Mr. Frank Barber. Finding him free, Mr. Wilkinson began, "Frank, we have a bit of a problem here. Are you aware of the situation with the Richards family?"

"Not only am I aware of it, I have been on the phone all day trying to stave off a future firestorm. I have already fielded several calls from the parents and their lawyer. I have been in consultation with district lawyers to see exactly how deep we are in here. Oh, and did I mention that they have contacted the media? At least three papers have already called—but I have been able to hold them off. Did I mention that Ashley is not in school today? Just exactly what have you gotten us into?" Principal Barber demanded.

This was the second time today that Mr. Wilkinson felt as though he had been slapped. "Whoa. Just wait one minute. I have been teaching this course for fifteen years without complaint. Please do not tell me that you are going to throw me under the bus for one complaint. You cannot be serious."

"Customer service," Principal Barber replied, "that is our business now."

"Look," Mr. Wilkinson relied, "I understand your position, and I apologize for the trouble and inconvenience that this situation has caused you, but public schools are places for the free exchange of ideas. Are we going to start banning and burning books now too?"

"Do not get melodramatic, Tim. I do not interfere with what goes on in your classroom, never have. Now. Let me do my job," Principal Barber stated.

"But, can we at least try to reason with the parents? Can we attempt a conference, with all of us present?" Mr. Wilkinson asked.

"I will see what I can do," Principal Barber replied. "I will try to give you a few days notice so that you can prepare. Now, please, let me get back to this. This is a real shit storm. I have more calls to make. This has the potential to end careers."

Mr. Wilkinson left the office in shock. He was incredulous that his field trip could warrant dissent from parents and negative media attention on his beloved community high school. He decided he would relax over the weekend and regroup. He pondered whether he should consult an attorney himself, but decided that he would revisit that question when he returned to work on Monday.

Mr. Wilkinson returned to work on Monday refreshed and optimistic about the situation with the Richards family. He was confident in the fact that he was a good teacher, and he was convinced that he could persuade the Richards family to allow Ashley to remain in his class.

However, this feeling quickly changed when Mr. Wilkinson checked his morning mail. On the top of his pile he found a note from Principal Barber indicating that the meeting with the Richards family was to take place that day during his planning period, just three hours away. Mr. Wilkinson felt fear flow through his entire body. How was he to prepare for this meeting when he had two courses to teach? How would he keep his composure?

At 9:50 am, Mr. Wilkinson entered the office of Principal Frank Barber. He fully expected Mr. Richards to already be there, but to his great relief he found only Frank. He entered the office and shut the door. Principal Frank Barber was seated behind his desk, and Mr. Wilkinson took a seat in one of two chairs across from the principal's desk. Principal Barber had agreed to host the conference in his office, but considered himself to be more of a silent witness, rather than mediator.

Mr. Wilkinson was anxious. This was the first time in his tenure that his pedagogy had been questioned in such a manner. He was accustomed to explaining his rationale to parents, but he had never experienced the silent vitriol of Mr. Richards via secondhand threats of lawyers and character assassination through the media.

Mr. Wilkinson wished desperately that the Richards family had allowed him to explain himself and the goals of his course. But, he was terrified at how a potential lawsuit and a media already unfriendly to teachers would paint him. He also worried about how his community, already Islamophobic and fueled by the media, would judge him. Perhaps the most crushing blow of this entire incident, Mr. Wilkinson had never experienced a parent who was so thoroughly unwilling to listen, particularly a parent of a student to whom he had thought he had made a connection.

Always comforted by knowledge, Mr. Wilkinson came armed with research suggesting the positive impact that instruction of religious diversity could have on students, which he was able to gather during two five-minute passing times between his first two classes. He also brought a copy of his syllabus and all of his course texts in order to demonstrate the fact that he was not attempting to endorse any one religion over another.

"Frank, I am so glad that you are alone," Mr. Wilkinson said soon after he sat down. "I thought we would have had more time to talk and discuss a strategy for how we would handle this conference. I thought you were going to give me a few days to prepare."

"That was the plan, but plans change," Principal Barber replied.

"Frank, you have my home number. Why didn't you call me and give me a head's up?" Mr. Wilkinson asked.

"The district lawyers advised against that, Tim. I'm sorry."

Mr. Wilkinson nodded knowingly. "So, do we have a plan?"

"Just remain calm and do not say anything controversial. We need to contain this," Principal Barber replied.

As if on command, Principal Barber's phone rang. He answered, and replied, "Yes, send him in." Without knocking, Mr. Richards entered the office. Principal Barber rose and shook hands with Mr. Richards. Mr. Wilkinson rose as well, but Mr. Richards did not accept Mr. Wilkinson's extended hand. Instead, he sat down and moved his chair away from the chair in which Mr. Wilkinson previously sat. Mr. Wilkinson sat down.

Principal Barber began, "Mr. Richards, thank you so much for coming today. We wish to hear all of your concerns, please." Both Principal Barber and Mr. Wilkinson looked at Mr. Richards.

Mr. Richards smiled, but looked only at Principal Barber, "My wife and I have raised our children to be faithful Christians and we cannot abide the liberal philosophy espoused by this *teacher*. He is ruining what we have established in our home." Mr. Wilkinson listened and tried to explain the rationale behind his field trips and his course in general. Each time he opened his mouth to speak, Mr. Richards interrupted, and refused to allow Mr. Wilkinson to finish a sentence.

Mr. Richards became agitated and said, "I do not want my child to look at the one true God as equivalent to the pagan beliefs espoused in this course. It will be over my dead body that my daughter learns anything about terrorist religions, and I want her out of this class! I have alerted the media and my attorney, as you well know, Mr. Barber. Please know that this will not stand, and this is not over. " He concluded the conference by getting up and slamming the door to the office.

Instruction about religion in general and the course on World Studies made Principal Frank Barber extremely nervous. Principal Barber believed that the Constitution requires that public schools be "religion-free zones." This problem was exacerbated by the predominately white, Baptist community of Spring Hills. Anti-Muslim sentiment and the intolerance made the news three years prior when members of the Baptist Church held signs outside of a mosque while people attended services. Signs read, "Mohammad is a false prophet" and "Mosques are monuments to terrorism!"

There was also an incident in the community of an assault on a Muslim male as the result of a parking dispute while members of the victim's family asserted it was a hate crime. The incident took place in a local mall.

The Muslim male had just pulled into a parking spot when two Caucasian males approached the car. As his family waited inside the car, he stepped out to find out what the two men wanted. As one of the males asked, "You are one of those terrorists aren't you?"

The other landed a punch to the Muslim man's abdomen and yelled, "You and your family need to go back to the desert!" As the children were crying in the car, the wife called the police. A report was filed, but no other action was taken, as the perpetrators were never found.

During the weeks that followed the failed parent conference, Mr. Richards gained much support for his views in the community and managed to get the issue on the next school board meeting agenda. Mr. Wilkinson was asked to attend in order to defend his course.

Mr. Wilkinson argued that Mr. Richards's fears were unwarranted. He stated, "Having taught world religion courses numerous times, I have never once seen a student abandon his or her current religion and adopt a new one as a result of the course. If anything, I have found that the study of world religions often deepens students' appreciation for their own traditions because they are able to understand their uniqueness."

The argument that all religions must be given "equal time" is reminiscent of previous arguments by creationists that biology classes must "teach the debate" between biological evolution and "intelligent design." These sorts of arguments are predicated on the assumption that students will select which religions and worldviews they will adopt.

During the board meeting, one parent stood up and said, "I wouldn't be upset if my kid learned more about a different religion. I'd be upset if they learned the same thing over and over and over again."

Mr. Wilkinson spoke, "To fail to teach about Islam to a generation whose lives have been shaped by the war on terror, a decade of American military presence in the Islamic world, and the Arab Spring is grossly irresponsible if not immoral."

Mr. Richards retorted, "I cannot believe the good people of Spring Hill agree with you, Mr. Wilkinson! To overstep the parents' rights to raise their children in their own faith by promoting the poisonous influence of terrorist religions is intolerable and unacceptable in this community. We will not sit back and allow this to happen!"

A petition signed by hundreds of members of the community was handed to the president of the school board. The petition requested that the World Studies course be removed from the school curriculum and that Mr. Wilkinson be dismissed for espousing liberal viewpoints and terrorist philosophies in his classroom.

The school board deliberated and returned with the suspension of all field trips to religious sites as part of the elective class in World Studies and a formal review of Mr. Wilkinson's teaching. In January of the following year, Spring Hills High School dropped the elective class in World Studies.

TEACHING NOTES

Religious freedom is one of the founding principles of the United States, protected by the First Amendment and other federal laws. The landmark Civil Rights Act of 1964 was enacted to prevent discrimination in federally funded programs, barring discrimination based on race, national origin, sex, and religion. Title IV of the Civil Rights Act of 1964 prohibits discrimination based on religion in public primary and secondary schools, as well as in public colleges and universities.

Public primary and secondary schools are open to all members of the public, regardless of their faith. Students should not face discrimination or harassment because of their religious backgrounds, their beliefs, their distinctive religious dress, or religious expression. Individual student expression may not be suppressed simply because it is religious.

The issue of the proper role of religion in the public schools continues to be the subject of great controversy. School officials, parents, and students, as well as lawyers and judges, wrestle with these questions every day. Decision makers must address many competing views and demands, and invariably looking to balance the constitutional mandates of the separation of church and state, and the right to freely exercise religion, as well as freedom of speech.

QUESTIONS FOR DISCUSSION

1. Discuss the role of religion in public school curriculum. What, if any, is its purpose?
2. In consideration of a common goal to ensure a vision that preserves religious liberty and upholds religious freedom for individuals, what is your opinion on the separation of church and state? What is your opinion on including religious doctrine in the school curriculum that may be contrary to parents' beliefs? Did the board make the correct decision? Explain your answer.
3. Did Principal Barber make the right decision in this case? What would you have done differently as an educational leader?
4. Is Mr. Wilkinson negligent in any way in this case? Explain your answer.
5. In light of the board's decision, what would you do next if you were Mr. Wilkinson?
6. Read *Lemon v Kurtzman* (1971) and familiarize yourself with the "*Lemon* test." A central element of that decision was that any religious activity must have a principal or primary effect that neither "advances

nor inhibits religion." What difficulties do we have maintaining a neutral public position on religion in schools?

7. Should Christian nativity displays be included in holiday observances at public schools or on the grounds? Defend your answer.

8. How can decision makers in education strive toward a vision of a pluralistic America that is open and welcoming to all groups, including religious minorities?

9. By what means can school districts set forth clear policies regarding religion in the public schools that satisfy both the letter and the spirit of the First Amendment?

ADDITIONAL ACTIVITIES

1. In *State of Tennessee v John Thomas Scopes* (1926), John Scopes, a biology teacher in Dayton, Tennessee, was charged with violating state law by teaching Darwin's theory of evolution. In 1925, the state legislature sanctioned that to teach any doctrine that denied creation as presented in the King James Version of the Bible as unlawful.

   The judge ruled out discussion of constitutional legality, and because Scopes had obviously taught Darwin's theory of evolution, he was convicted and fined. On appeal to the Supreme Court, the constitutionality of the state's law was upheld, but Scopes was acquitted on the technicality that he had been fined excessively.

   The law was repealed in 1967. However, Christian fundamentalists in the United States continue to campaign for a return to creationist teaching (Ginger, 1974). Read the *State of Tennessee v John Thomas Scopes* (1926) and discuss parallels to this case.

   If the Scopes trial took place today, how would the outcome be different? What policies are in place now that would help or hinder John Thomas Scopes?

   A teacher can be dismissed for reasons specified in school codes that have nothing to do with teaching such as moral turpitude, insubordination, or willful misconduct; how can we ensure due process for Mr. Wilkinson in this case?

2. In the landmark case *Abington v Schempp* (1963), which banned Bible reading or prayer in public schools as unconstitutional, Justice Thomas Clark remarked, "It might well be said that one's education is not complete without a study of comparative religion or the history of religion and its advancement of civilization" (p. 374).

   This distinction between the state-sponsored practice of a religion and teaching about religion has been reiterated in subsequent decisions (*Edwards v Aquillard*, 1987; *Stone v Graham*, 1980). Furthermore, in the state of West Virginia, the world history standards require students to learn about major religions and their philosophies.

While the controversial course at Spring Hills was an elective, every student in the state is mandated to learn about different religious traditions. Read these cases and review these standards. After so doing, does your opinion on this case change? Discuss in small groups.

3. In *Wisconsin v Yoder* (1972), Chief Justice Warren Burger argued that parents have a "fundamental right" to guide the religious future of their children. However, a democratic society must also educate students to have moral agency and to think for themselves about big questions, such as those involving religion.

   Any right of parents to guide their children's values cannot justify preventing students from receiving accurate and useful information about other religions. Read *Wisconsin v Yoder* and after so doing, reflect on whether your opinion on this case has changed. Discuss in small groups.

REFERENCES

Bandura, A., Caprara, G. V., Barbaranelli, C., Pastorelli, C., & Regalia, C. (2001). Sociocognitive self-regulatory mechanisms governing transgressive behavior. *Journal of Personality and Social Psychology, 80*(1), 125–35.

Baumeister, R. F., Zhang, L., & Vohs, K. D. (2004). Gossip as cultural learning. *Review of General Psychology, 8*(2), 111–21.

Caprara, G. V., Tisak, M. S., Alessandri, G., Fontaine, R. G., Fida, R., & Paciello, M. (2014). The contribution of moral disengagement in mediating individual tendencies toward aggression and violence. *Developmental Psychology, 50*(1), 71–85.

Edwards v Aguillard, 482 U.S. 578 (1987).

Ginger, R. (1974). *Six days or forever? Tennessee v. John Thomas Scopes*. New York, NY: Oxford University Press.

Lemon v Kurtzman, 403 U.S. 602 (1971).

Stone v Graham, 499 U.S. 39 (1980).

Wachlin, M., & Johnson, B. R. (2005). What do American teens know about the Bible? *The Bible literacy report: What do American teens need to know and what do they know?* New York, NY: Bible Literacy Project, Inc.

Wisconsin v Yoder, 406 U.S. 205 (1972).

Chapter Six

Common Errors? Language Diversity in Schools

What Should a Leader Do?

INTRODUCTION

As the United States becomes increasingly multicultural, cultural competence and the ability to effectively lead and advocate for an array of diverse students and their families is a requirement of twenty-first century leaders. This case has been written to reflect the need for educational leaders to create and sustain a school culture and instructional programs conducive to student learning through collaboration, trust, and a personalized learning environment with high expectations for students.

Sometimes, the creation of such a climate involves difficult conversations and questioning practices that are not culturally responsive. More specifically, this case deals with language prejudice based upon adult lack of knowledge of language traditions. The reader is left with the dilemma: how should a new leader disrupt inequitable practices within a school without alienating the staff?

In terms of background for this case, Black English, Ebonics, African American English, African American Language (AAL), and African American Vernacular are just some of the terms used to describe the same language tradition. This language tradition has been renamed over the decades to combat the disparagement that often comes to be associated with it; as each new and improved version is coined, some way is found to condemn it. To combat this negativity, terms have been coined such as "Soul talk," "Black talk," and "heritage language."

Background of African American Language: The King Case, 1979

In *Martin Luther King Junior Elementary School Children v Ann Arbor School District Board*, the parents of African American students in a pre-dominantly white school contended that African American students in general and AAL-speaking students in particular were being systematically placed in special education programs and were generally seen by their teachers as uneducable because of their perceived lack of language skills.

Geneva Smitherman, a University of Michigan professor, linguist, and consultant for the plaintiffs in the case, notes that the case was the "first test of the applicability of 1703(f), the language provision of the 1974 Equal Educational Opportunity Act, to Black English speakers" (1999, p. 132). The case was also a crucible for the notion that the language African American children acquire before they go to school constitutes a "home language" that is different enough from Standard English that it can be a barrier to their educational achievement.

On July 12, 1979, the court found that the Ann Arbor School District violated the students' right to equal educational opportunity. The institutional response to Black English was found to be the main barrier (Smitherman, 1999).

By not bridging the divide between the students' home language (AAL) and the Standard English that the teachers were using, teachers were denying these students the education that they came to school to attain. Some teachers dismissed the students as ignorant or uneducable because of cultural assumptions about their language use. Unfortunately, such attitudes still exist, particularly with those who have not had contact with non-standard varieties of English in any sustained or systematic way.

Background of African American Language: Oakland, CA, 1996

The "Ebonics issue" was revisited in the mainstream media in the mid-1990s, when the Oakland School Board, in an effort to address the achievement gap between their white and Black students, focused on the issue of language. As Smitherman (1999) argues, "Oakland's contention was that the students' dismal levels of educational achievement were attributable, in great measure, to the significant linguistic mismatch between the home and school commu-nication systems. To reduce this mismatch and its consequent impact on literacy and academic performance, Oakland proposed to implement a bilin-gual/bicultural language pedagogy" (p. 150). This pedagogy, influenced by a number of leading scholars, emphasized that students whose home language were not Standard English should be able to use their home languages in school, and that teachers could use them as a bridge while teaching students

Standard English. Essentially, the practice of "code switching" would be normalized within schools.

However, instead of focusing on the issue of helping students learn, the media instead focused on the word Ebonics (Ebony + phonics or "black sounds"), which led many to believe that the board called for teachers to actually teach Ebonics to students (when the actual resolution was to acknowledge that Ebonics was these students' first language). The national attention of the Oakland case was unfortunately squandered by a national media unwilling to acknowledge language differences in an increasingly culturally and linguistically segregated society.

The King and Oakland cases illustrate that AAL is a legitimate—not "broken" or "lazy"—variety of English. There are features of AAL (both grammatical and rhetorical) that, without specific knowledge of, white teachers are likely to misinterpret, the results of which can have longstanding consequences not only in the communication between these teachers and their students, but on the esteem and engagement of the students themselves.

Addressing the Cultural and Linguistic Mismatch

Even as teachers attempt to treat all of their students equally, they overlook the disparities in cultural capital between standard and non-standard speaking students. Because many white teachers, as members of the dominant discourse community, have been culturally influenced to profess that race makes no difference, many do not naturally realize that, in fact, it does.

Instead of ignoring these differences in an effort to treat students "the same no matter what their color," we need to overtly acknowledge that cultural differences exist and that they can have an effect on how learning and teaching happens and should happen. As Delpit (1988) maintains, "it is impossible to create a model for the good teacher without taking issues of culture and community context into account" (p. 291). To assert "I do not see color" is a culturally irresponsible position to take and does not serve our students well.

Colorblind and colormute ideologies condemn any words or language that may relate, signify, or give meaning to race; in reality, they perpetuate racism, the myth of meritocracy, and denials of institutional or structural inequality. According to Charity Hudley and Mallinson (2011), "Most people would find it difficult to accept a message, even an indirect message, that they have to suppress part of their linguistic identity to operate within mainstream culture. African Americans, with their specific social and cultural history, often live this reality every day" (p. 74). Teachers who have not been trained in critical literacy practices and/or are a part of the hegemonic majority and have not questioned issues of power and authority and their impact on literacy and students may not feel they are doing anything wrong when they perceive home languages to be deficient and deem them as subordinate, something to be disciplined, corrected, altered.

In fact, this type of disciplinary knowledge, a "pedagogy of telling" (Sizer, 1984), deems knowledge as a direct transfer from teacher to student, with no exchange, no inter-play, no struggle for common ground, no joint knowledge construction.

Many current teachers are already questioning their own hegemonic worldviews and training, especially when what they have been taught does not work in their diverse, multicultural classrooms. According to Brock, Parks, and Moore (2004), "The challenge, then, is to help students attain multiple literacies by exploring the literacy customs and practices from which they come, as well as the literacy practices of the dominant culture" (p. 27). In order to make this happen, more training for teachers to examine their own attitudes about culture and diversity is crucial to facilitate change (Diller, 2004).

As educators, we must do better to address student racial and cultural alienation in school. And while organizations like the National Council of Teachers of English, the Conference on College Composition and Communication, and the Linguistic Society of America have drafted and passed multiple resolutions on the importance of teachers addressing differences in multicultural home languages that students bring to class, the disconnect between theory and practice continues, to the detriment of students.

Widespread effort must be made to educate teachers from the beginning of their careers about the impact that culture has on language and learning, and the need to take it into consideration when working with students not well versed in Standard English. According to Smitherman (2000), "Language is the foundation stone of education and the medium of instruction in all subjects and disciplines throughout schooling. It is critical that teachers have an understanding of and appreciation for the language students bring to school" (p. 119). In short, we must acknowledge and embrace language differences in order to educate all of our students; to give them the same access to education does not mean we must treat them exactly the same.

THE CASE

> We die. That may be the meaning of life. . . . But we do language. That may be
> the measure of our lives.
> –Toni Morrison

As a young undergraduate student, Mr. Delisep was lucky enough to have one professor, Professor Lamb, who tried her hardest to teach her students that "Black English," as she called it, or AAL, as it is currently deemed, was a valid language in its own right and did not signify a deficiency of the mouths, minds, or ideas of the people who spoke it. Professor Lamb would always say, "We must be language activists."

Mr. Delisep knew this early on. But what did that mean for an English teacher? Never a grammarian, Mr. Delisep had trouble with linguistics and modern English grammar, both taught by the same strict and gruff professor, Dr. Abramowicz, but the one thing this professor taught him was, "anything goes in informal language, as long as one is understood."

Mr. Delisep started his career teaching English in the Central Orange School District. After his second year, large demographic shifts led to major changes; a neighboring school district closed and all of the students were sent to various schools within the Central Orange School District. The now de-funct East Orange School District had a predominantly African American population, making Central Orange School District much more diverse very quickly.

In his third year, Mr. Delisep's classes changed from predominantly white to racially diverse. Mr. Delisep began to hear different language pat-terns in his classes and in the hallways, as home languages were used. He would hear his colleagues complain about "non-Standard English" being used and negative perceptions of the students who used it, but Mr. Delisep largely stayed out of these conversations, for his knowledge as a young teacher only went so far.

He was living and working within the larger, more dominant white Eng-lish teacher hegemony where there was only one right way. He did not believe there was intentional stripping of language and culture, but he was unsure about how to have these conversations with his peers.

Many of his peers did not understand that AAL possesses its own gram-mar, syntax, and conventions, and those who speak it do so not because they do not know any better, but because this is the historical language of their own, their home language, both literally and figuratively.

After ten years of teaching English, Mr. Delisep became an assistant principal at another high school in the Central Orange School District. Upon his arrival at Emily Dickinson High School, he saw that the English teachers were wearing Emily Dickinson High School English department t-shirts that also listed their grammatical pet peeves regarding student writing.

Some of these phrases, or "errors," as they deemed them, were AAL conventions. Mr. Delisep was immediately put off by this "t-shirt debacle," as he deemed it, yet he was hesitant to make this his first charge as a new educational leader in this school that was also new to him.

New to both his profession as an administrator and to this building, he questioned what to do, particularly when he learned that the English depart-ment proudly wore these T-shirts every Friday for several years. This was a cultural norm within the school. Perhaps the most culturally non-responsive "grammar peeve," was the last one to "grace" the shirt. It displayed the

ignorance of the all-white English department of the AAL grammar rule, the
Habitual Be. The Habitual Be is defined as the use on an uninflected "be,"
marking habitual or extended actions.

During his school tour during his first week, Mr. Delisep noticed a sign
hanging in the hallway, near the entrance to the English department wing. It
read:

EDHS English Department's Grammar Peeves:
Just say no to irregardless.
Their There They're—get it right.
Loose and Lose are two different words.
It's is short for It Is and its means belonging to it.
Apostrophes don't make plurals.
Your and You're—there is a difference.
You didn't seen anything—you saw it.
Your stupid! My stupid what?
Verbs have—not has—to agree with their subjects.
Don't use no double negatives.
You do not: "ax someone a question." You ask someone a question.
She always be here—be is not a verb by itself.

Mr. Delisep knew that some white teachers would get offended if their
students thought them racist before they got to know them. This never both-
ered him. His philosophy was that it is not the students' jobs to accept their
teachers without question. Rather, it is the teachers' charge to get students to
want to learn, and teachers should also be open to learning from their students.

Mr. Delisep wondered how the sign and the t-shirts would make the
African American students in the school feel. He decided that he would
politely ask the head of the English department about the origins of the t-shirt
and the sign.

Ms. Chapman was a thirty-year veteran English teacher at EDHS, having
spent her entire career in the same building and the same room. Tall, sophis-
ticated, and fashionable, Ms. Chapman brought an air of mystery to the
English department. Mr. Delisep knocked on the open door.

Ms. Chapman looked up and smiled. Mr. Delisep entered the room cautiously and looked around. Art prints, couches, pillows, and floor lamps
graced the open space. A stage was the focal point at the front of the room. "I
do not believe we have met," Ms. Chapman smiled as she extended her hand.
"I am Julia Chapman, English and drama."

"Marcus Delisep. Brand new principal, assistant principal rather, second
day."

"Welcome Marcus, uh, may I call you Marcus? You know how some administrators can be, even though I think I may be old enough to be your mother," Ms. Chapman mused.

"Marcus is fine," Mr. Delisep replied. "Listen," he continued, "I was just taking a bit of a walking tour, getting my bearings, and I noticed your English department sign." Ms. Chapman looked confused. "Out in the hallway?" Mr. Delisep asked.

"Oh, that old thing" Ms. Chapman said. "Yes. A couple of us made that years ago. We made t-shirts too. Raggedy old things now. People still wear them though, except me," Ms. Chapman replied.

"Hmm," Mr. Delisep thought. "I am wondering what message you think the sign, and the t-shirts, send to the students," he asked.

"Well, you know I never thought about it," Ms. Chapman replied, "it was just our little English department joke."

TEACHING NOTES

As the United States becomes increasingly multicultural, cultural competence and the ability to effectively lead and advocate for an array of diverse students and their families is a requirement of twenty-first century leaders. This case has been written to reflect Educational Leadership Constituent Council Standard 2.0:

> A building-level education leader applies knowledge that promotes the success of every student by sustaining a school culture and instructional program conducive to student learning through collaboration, trust, and a personalized learning environment with high expectations for students; creating and evaluating a comprehensive, rigorous and coherent curricular and instructional school program; developing and supervising the instructional and leadership capacity of school staff; and promoting the most effective and appropriate technologies to support teaching and learning within a school environment. (Educational Leadership Constituent Council, 2011, p. 10)

This standard was informed by research that emphasized the critical importance of understanding how diversity affects the learning process and how school culture can be used to influence student success.

Cultural competence is a developmental process that occurs along a continuum. There are six possibilities, starting from one end and building toward the other: 1) cultural destructiveness, 2) cultural incapacity, 3) cultural blindness, 4) cultural pre-competence, 5) cultural competency, and 6) cultural proficiency (Cross, Bazron, Dennis, & Isaacs, 1989). It is very important for educators to assess where they fall along the continuum.

A culturally competent school is defined as one that honors, respects, and values diversity in theory and in practice, and where teaching and learning are reflective of various cultures and made relevant and meaningful to students from different backgrounds (Klotz, 2006). Cultural competence is having an awareness of one's own cultural identity and mindfulness about the differences in others, and the ability to effectually interact with cultural groups of students and their families.

It is the capacity to appreciate the within-group differences that make each student unique, while recognizing, celebrating, and incorporating diversity in programs, curriculum, and instructional practices. This understanding informs and expands teaching practices in the culturally competent educator's classroom. Cultural competence facilitates understanding, communication with, and effective interaction with people across cultures (Stavans, 2001).

Cultural competence is defined as a set of congruent behaviors, attitudes, and policies that come together in a system, agency, or among professionals and enables that system, agency, or those professionals to work effectively in cross-cultural situations (Cross, Bazron, Dennis, & Isaacs, 1989; Isaacs & Benjamin, 1991). Operationally defined, cultural competence is the integration and transformation of knowledge about individuals and groups of people into specific standards, policies, practices, and attitudes used in appropriate cultural settings to increase the quality of services, thereby producing better outcomes (Davis, 1997).

The word *culture* implies the integrated patterns of human behavior that include thoughts, communications, actions, customs, beliefs, values, and institutions of racial, ethnic, religious, or social groups.

The word *competence* implies having the capacity to function within the context of culturally integrated patterns of human behavior defined by a group (Cross, Bazron, Dennis, & Isaacs, 1989). Having the capacity to function effectively in other cultural contexts requires individuals to develop new patterns of behavior and then to successfully apply them in the appropriate settings.

All of these factors impact leadership. Ryan (2006) defines inclusive leadership as "not just the process of leadership that is inclusive; the ends of the process are also geared toward inclusion. Inclusive leadership aims to achieve inclusion in all aspects of schooling and beyond the school to the local and global community" (p. 18).

The process of cultural competence involves uncovering one's own biases and prejudices, developing cross-cultural skills, and continuous critical reflective practice (Kumagai & Lypson, 2009). Organizations must have a defined set of values and principles, and demonstrate behaviors, attitudes, policies, and structures that enable them to work effectively cross-culturally.

The pedagogical capacity to support diversity in schools is a developmental process that involves substantial learning about pedagogy and instructional design to support diversity and involves practice and reflection to support positive outcomes (Krutky, 2008). Educators with the skills, knowledge, and attitudes to value the diversity among students will contribute to an educational system designed to serve all students well. See Cross, Bazron, Dennis, and Isaacs (1989); Isaacs and Benjamin (1991); Davis (1997); National Education Association (n.d.); and Trumbull and Pacheco (2005) for additional information on cultural competence.

There are five components that contribute to a school's ability to become more culturally competent. The system should 1) value diversity, 2) have the capacity for cultural self-assessment, 3) be conscious of the "dynamics" inherent when cultures interact, 4) institutionalize cultural knowledge, and 5) develop adaptations to service delivery reflecting an understanding of diversity between and within cultures. Further, these five elements must be ingrained in every aspect of the school and reflected in attitudes, structures, policies, and services (Cross, Bazron, Dennis, & Isaacs, 1989).

There are four cognitive components related to cultural competence (Moule, 2012).

1. *Awareness* is consciousness of one's personal reactions to people who are different. A teacher who recognizes that s/he profiles students with limited English proficiency as slow has cultural awareness of her/his reactions to this group of people.
2. *Attitude* emphasizes the difference between training that increases awareness of cultural bias and beliefs in general and training that has participants carefully examine their own beliefs and values about cultural differences. Our values and beliefs about equality may be inconsistent with our behaviors, and we may be unaware of it.
3. *Knowledge* plays an important part of cultural competence development. Awareness and understanding of the norms and differences between groups allows educators to better meet the needs of students. Being able to see situations through different lenses allows us to better support the learning process.
4. The *Skills* component focuses on practicing cultural competence. Cultural competence is a developmental process where individuals and organizations can develop various levels of awareness, knowledge, and skills to meet the needs of students. Knowledge-based skills are necessary for educators to provide environments conducive to student learning.

We emphasize the need for educators to provide an environment of respect and reciprocity of ideas and provide the mechanism for educators to learn how to teach students from different backgrounds. Cultural competence is both a moral and ethical responsibility, as is creating a welcoming environment for students to succeed. Incorporating racial and ethnic minority contributions in curriculum and diversifying pedagogical practices can dramatically improve our educational system and student outcomes (Bauman, Bustillos, Bensimon, Brown, & Bartee, 2005).

QUESTIONS FOR DISCUSSION

1. What role should Mr. Delisep play in this case? Should the principal step in? Should Mr. Delisep do something about the t-shirts and the sign, or should he simply report his concerns to the principal? Explain your answers.
2. What proactive steps could have been taken within the school community to prepare teachers for a more diverse student population?
3. How can the issue of professional development play a role for all of the characters in this case?
4. What role should cultural competency play in the lives and teachers, administrators, and school districts in general?
5. What can be done to increase cultural competency within schools and districts? Can should be done in the case of Central Orange School District?
6. What should Mr. Delisep do in this case as an inclusive leader without alienating his staff? What would you do?

ADDITIONAL ACTIVITIES

Look up the phenomenon of "code switching." How can code switching be taught and/or utilized in schools in ways that honor the home languages of students? Create a plan to implement this pedagogical practice, and share in small groups.

REFERENCES

Banks, J. A. (2007). *Educating citizens in a multicultural society.* New York, NY: Teachers College Press.
Banks, J. (2013). Group identity and citizenship education in global times. *Kappa Delta Pi Record, 49*(3), 108–12.
Bauman, G. L., Bustillos, L. T., Bensimon, M., & Brown II, C., & Bartee, R. D. (2005). *Achieving equitable educational outcomes with all students: The institution's roles and responsibilities.* Washington, DC: Association of American Colleges and Universities. http://www.aacu.org/sites/default/files/files/mei/bauman_et_al.pdf.
Brock, C. H., Parks, L. A., & Moore, D. K. (2004). Literacy, learning, and language variation: Implications for instruction. In F. B. Boyd, C. H. Brock, & M. S. Rozendal. *Multicultural*

and multilinguial literacy and language: Contexts and practices (pp. 15–31). New York, NY: The Guilford Press.

Cross T., Bazron, B., Dennis, K., & Isaacs, M. (1989). *Towards a culturally competent system of care, volume I.* Washington, DC: Georgetown University Child Development Center, CASSP Technical Assistance Center.

Charity Hudley, A. H., & Mallinson, C. (2012). *Understanding English language variation in U.S. schools.* New York, NY: Teachers College Press.

Conference on College Composition and Communication. (1974). Students' right to their own language position statement. In *Special Issue of CCC XXV.* http://www.ncte.org/library/NCTEFiles/Groups/CCCC/NewSRTOL.pdf.

Davis, K. (1997). Exploring the intersection between cultural competency and managed behavioral health care policy: Implications for state and county mental health agencies. Alexandria, VA: National Technical Assistance Center for State Mental Health Planning.

Delpit, L. (1988). The silenced dialogue: Pedagogy and power in educating other people's children. *Harvard Educational Review, 58,* 280–98.

Delpit, L. (2002). No kinda sense. In L. Delpit & J. K. Dowdy (Eds.), *The skin that we speak,* (pp. 31–48). New York, NY: The New Press.

Diller, D. (2004). Learning to look through a new lens: One teacher's reflection on the change process as related to cultural awareness. In F. B. Boyd, C. H. Brock, M. S. Rozendal (Eds.), *Multicultural and multilingual literacy and language* (pp. 77–92). New York, NY: Guilford Press.

Educational Leadership Constituent Council. (2011). Educational Leadership Program Standards. *National Policy Board for Educational Administration.* http://www.ncate.org/LinkClick.aspx?fileticket=zRZI73R0nOQ%3D&tabid=676.

Isaacs, M., & Benjamin, M. (1991). *Towards a culturally competent system of care, volume II, programs which utilize culturally competent principles.* Washington, DC: Georgetown University Child Development Center, CASSP Technical Assistance Center.

Klotz, M. B. (2006, March). Culturally competent schools: Guidelines for secondary school principals. *Student Counseling.* National Association of School Psychologists. http://www.nasponline.org/resources/principals/Culturally%20Competent%20Schools%20NASSP.pdf.

Kohl, H. (1994). *I won't learn from you and other thoughts on creative maladjustment.* New York, NY: The New Press.

Krutky, J. B. (2008). *Effective practices for academic leaders: Intercultural competency – preparing students to be global citizens The Baldwin-Wallace experience (effective practices for academic leaders archive).* Sterling, VA: Stylus Publishing.

Kumagai, A. K., & Lypson, M. L. (2009). Beyond cultural competence: Critical consciousness, social justice, and multicultural education. *U.S. National Library of Medicine National Institutes of Health, 84*(6), 782–87.

Moule, J. (2012). *Cultural competence: A primer for educators.* Belmont, CA: Wadsworth/Cengage.

Morrison, T. (1993). *Nobel lecture.* The Nobel Foundation. http://www.nobelprize.org/nobel_prizes/literature/laureates /1993/morrison-lecture.html.

National Education Association. (n.d.). Diversity toolkit: Class and income. http://www.nea.org/tools/18836.htm.

Nieto, S. (2013). Diversity, globalization, and education: What do they mean for teachers and teacher educators? *Kappa Delta Pi Record, 49*(3), 105–07.

Rodriguez, G. M. (2013). Power and agency in education: Exploring the pedagogical dimensions of funds of knowledge. *Review of Research in Education, 37,* 87–120.

Ryan, J. (2006). *Inclusive leadership.* San Francisco, CA: Jossey-Bass.

Salazar, M. (2013). A humanizing pedagogy: Reinventing the principles and practice of education as a journey toward liberation. *Review of Research in Education, 37,* 121–48.

Sizer, T. R. (1984). *Horace's compromise: The dilemma of the American high school.* Boston, MA: Houghton Mifflin.

Smitherman, G. (1999, February). CCCC's role in the struggle for language rights. *College Composition and Communication, 50*(3), 349–76.

Smitherman, G. (2000). *Talkin that talk: Language, culture and education in African America.* New York, NY: Routledge.

Smitherman, G. (2006). *Word from the mother: Language and African Americans.* New York, NY: Routledge.

Stavans, I. (2001). *The Hispanic condition: The power of a people* (2nd ed.). New York, NY: Harper Perennial.

Sue, D. W., Torino, G. C., Capodilupo, C. M., & Rivera, D. P. (2009). How white faculty perceive and react to different dialogues on race: Implications for education and training. *The Counseling Psychologist, 37*(8), 1090–115.

Trumbull, E. & Pacheco, M. (2005). *Leading with diversity: Cultural competence for teacher preparation and professional development.* Providence, RI: The Education Alliance at Brown University. http://files.eric.ed.gov/fulltext/ED494221.pdf.

Chapter Seven

The Summer Slide

Cultural Conflict

INTRODUCTION

This case describes the summer slide, or what happens when students refrain from reading and other academic pursuits during the summer months. Students who do not read over the summer will lose more than two months of reading achievement (Reading is Fundamental, n.d.). Summer reading loss is cumulative. By the end of sixth grade, children who consistently lose reading skills over cumulative summers will be two years behind their classmates.

This case makes mention of the term "white flight," which pertains to a phenomenon, originating in the mid-twentieth century United States, involving large-scale migrations of whites from racially diverse urban areas to more racially homogeneous suburban areas.

This case focuses on Mr. Bell, one of two African American teachers in an urban elementary school with a predominantly African American student population. Mr. Bell faces many challenges as a first-year teacher in an at-risk urban school. His desire to provide the best education for his students meant determining how to raise his students' skills in reading and math to get them on par with their peers at other schools in the state. Throughout the case, Mr. Bell finds himself in a position of convincing his colleagues to change their perceptions about the students and their parents.

THE CASE

John Dewey Elementary School is considered to be an "at-risk" urban school. It has been deemed as "failing" by the state and has been scheduled for reorganization and potentially state takeover, or closing. The majority of the kindergarten through sixth-grade student population do not meet the minimum grade-level proficiency standards in math and reading. Most students, 89 percent, are considered to be "struggling readers." The "summer slide" is a phenomenon that greatly impacts this student population.

In the 1960s and 1970s, John Dewey was a progressive magnet school in Philadelphia, with an emphasis on fine arts. In its heyday, John Dewey Elementary School prided itself on racial integration. Pulling students from highly segregated local public schools, it was seen as a bastion of social justice and the solution to the widening racial opportunity gaps that many low-income African American students faced in their more segregated schools. Highly competitive, John Dewey turned away many eligible candidates for sheer lack of resources. Then came white flight.

Beginning in the late 1980s, John Dewey was a shadow of its former glory. In a constant state of disrepair, John Dewey no longer takes applications for the most prestigious students. Currently, the school struggles to survive with competition from charter schools and a declining student population. The majority of students currently attending John Dewey do so because it is the closest school to their homes. Most students, 94 percent, are on free and reduced lunch.

The majority of teachers at John Dewey are new and seeking certification. Teacher morale is low because of low pay, lack of administrative support, and lack of resources. If teachers last more than one year, it is an accomplishment. Ill trained and ill equipped to work with students living in poverty, 75 percent of the teachers leave John Dewey annually.

Most teachers do not last even one full year. Some classes are taught entirely by a steady stream of substitutes. A recent newspaper article deemed John Dewey Elementary School an "Apartheid School," a metaphor for schools that disadvantage students of the highest need.

With a student population of 691, there are twenty-three teachers employed at John Dewey Elementary School. Class size is thirty students, which is not perceived to be optimal for student success and overall engagement, particularly for struggling students and those behind grade level in math and reading. Twenty-one teachers at John Dewey are white; two are African American. The entire student population is African American.

Ms. Williams and Mr. Bell both teach fifth grade at John Dewey Elementary School.

Mr. Bell attends a state university in the area and is himself a graduate of John Dewey, and one of two African American teachers working at John Dewey. A lifelong resident of the area, Mr. Bell received emergency certification from the district in order to meet the urgent need to fill the teaching vacancies of the school.

Ms. Williams is a recent graduate of a prestigious Ivy League teacher preparation program focusing on urban schools. Ms. Williams moved into an adjacent neighborhood in order to serve her required two years in a "high need" district, as stipulated by her certification program.

Ms. Williams and Mr. Bell are both novice second-grade teachers in the school. Mr. Bell has been assigned Ms. Williams as his mentor teacher. Both were hired on the day before school began in the fall, with no orientation, guidance, or formal introduction to the other faculty and staff members. Both scrambled to make it through their first day of school, having only hours the night before to piece together lesson plans and materials gleaned from their respective teacher education programs.

On the second day of school, Mr. Bell was informed that he was required to meet weekly with Ms. Williams to receive mentoring and teaching advice. During their common planning time, he knocked tentatively on her door. Ms. Williams answered the door, appearing frazzled. "Yes?"

"Hello, Ms. Williams. I apologize if this is a bad time. My name is Duane Bell. I am a new teacher this year, and you have been assigned as my mentor. I have my planning period now, and I wanted to come and introduce myself and ask when we might establish a common meeting time. I thought you had specials now. Was I wrong?"

"Well," Ms. Summer replied, "the students should be in art right now, but they have behaved so badly today that I am holding them back from art, recess, and anything else I can think of until they complete their homework, which was due this morning.

I know I am new here, but I cannot believe the students did not—or could not—complete the small literacy interest survey I sent home for homework last night. I even sent home a parent letter along with it with a corresponding questionnaire for the parents to complete. I only received one parent questionnaire, somewhat completed, but no student homework. Choices and consequences: that is my philosophy."

Mr. Bell looked into the room, which was now silent. All the students were looking at him. This saddened Mr. Bell. Not many years ago, he was a student in this class, and he could picture how this punishment would make him feel. Mr. Bell smiled, "How about we meet after school and we can discuss a good time for both of us to meet?" Ms. Williams agreed.

As he walked slowly down the hall back to his own classroom, Mr. Bell contemplated the situation. He knew that the students meant no disrespect. They were not accustomed to being asked to do homework, and, if they were, the constant revolving door of substitutes would never remember to collect it, let alone grade it.

A new teacher himself, Mr. Bell pondered what to do. He did not agree with the pedagogical philosophies of many of the teachers with whom he currently worked. Although this was only the second day of school, he overheard talk in the teacher's lounge and in the hallways, and he believed that the majority of his colleagues viewed the students from a deficit perspective, where adults pathologize their students, viewing them not for their strengths, but only for their weaknesses.

Mr. Bell remembered attending a segregated school in the late 1970s for kindergarten and first grade. His experiences were not great. He remembered his teacher, Mrs. Evans, his teacher for both grades, referring to him and his classmates as "you people," and feeling that he and his peers always disappointed her.

He felt neither valued nor smart in her classroom, but it was not until years later, while taking teacher certification courses, that he learned of Herbert Kohl's concept of "not learning" (Kohl, 1994). Then it all made sense. Kohl's concept of "not learning" involves the conscious or unconscious unwillingness to learn from a teacher who does not value one's identity.

Although unable to articulate such feelings at a young age, Mr. Bell did not communicate his dislike for school to his parents. His parents were aware that something was amiss. They immediately looked into other public school options for their son, who already excelled in art and music, and found John Dewey.

They submitted an application, and their son was accepted for second grade. Mr. Bell completed the rest of his elementary education at John Dewey, where he was exposed to cutting edge and arts-based pedagogies. It was also there that he experienced his first Black teacher, Mr. Johnson, and fell in love with learning.

Mr. Johnson was the first African American teacher that Mr. Bell had. Mr. Bell remembered Mr. Johnson's second-grade class as a transformational experience. Mr. Johnson still worked at the school, now as a fifth-grade teacher. Mr. Bell was confused as to why Mr. Johnson was not named as his mentor. As a new and yet uncertified teacher, Mr. Bell had been hesitant to question this, but he knew he had to speak with Mr. Johnson about the changes in the school and seek his advice on his best course of action.

At the end of the day, Mr. Bell knocked on the door of Mr. Johnson's classroom—the very same classroom where he fell in love with learning all of those years before. Mr. Johnson remembered his student Duane Bell from thirty-five years prior and happily shepherded him into the room.

Mr. Bell began the meeting by sharing his recent experiences at John Dewey and by communicating his dismay at having another first-year teacher, and one having little knowledge of the community, be assigned as his mentor.

Mr. Johnson did not waste any time mincing words, "Let me stop you right there. That is not your immediate fight. Your immediate fight is taking care of the children in your classroom. The other is a systemic fight; and, as a first-year teacher, you need to slow down. Take things one battle at a time.

You first need to center your children. Let them know you care. Then, get the trust of the parents.

These parents no longer trust this school. Once you secure their trust, then they will advocate for you. You cannot do this alone. You need the community, the school needs the community, and the community needs the school. But this is going to take some time.

A lot of bad things have happened within this school. There has been a breach of trust. And this is not a one-or two-year proposition. There is no quick fix here. If you are willing to commit, then I will help you. But, if you are just biding your time until a better job comes along, then . . . I cannot waste my time on you. So, I ask you: can I count on you? Can *we* count on you?"

Mr. Bell did not hesitate. "Yes. You can count on me. My students can count on me, and the community can as well. I just need some advice. You changed my world. How can I do the same for my students?"

Mr. Johnson sighed. "I am not sure. As you can see, this place has changed a lot since you were here. It has been tough being 'the only,' which I have been for quite some time. I see my colleagues come and go, and I have witnessed the ways in which teachers have ceased to believe in the kids who attend this school. In all honesty, I was hoping *you* would inspire me."

Mr. Bell left the meeting discouraged, but not dissuaded. Still a university student and possessing many good relationships with his professors, he immediately went to his university mentors for help.

He reached out to Dr. Diaz who chastised him a bit for forgetting himself and his community, "What do you mean you need advice on what to do? This is where you come from. You know these parents care about their children and the education of their children. Those were your parents at one time. Remember. Your community has funds of knowledge that you need to tap into. Bring the community into the school. Make it work."

Dr. Diaz provided Mr. Bell with some resources and materials, but Mr. Bell had some thinking to do. He knew that he needed to do a few things. First, he needed to provide the best education he could for the students in his classroom. This first meant figuring out how to raise his students' skills in reading and math to get them on par with their peers at other schools in the state.

Second, he needed to create an after-school program to assist not only his students but also the other students in the school to that same end, and eventually to create a companion program during the summer to combat the summer slide, so that when his students returned to school the next fall they would not be even further behind their peers in neighboring suburban schools.

Third, he needed to convince his colleagues that the students at John Dewey were capable and that their parents cared about them. He knew that he could accomplish the first, and maybe the second, but he was not sure about the third.

Mr. Bell thought back to his parents, who rarely entered the schoolhouse door but valued the education of their children, expecting them all to graduate and then attend college. Mr. Bell's parents did not want to interfere with the job the teachers were doing. They felt that the teachers should be able to do their jobs—without the interference of "busybody" parents.

In fact, Mr. and Mrs. Bell trusted their children's teachers implicitly. How this got twisted into "parents don't care," Mr. Bell was not sure. But, he felt that his story about why his parents did not directly involve themselves in the school could help his colleagues understand the parents of the students that they were currently teaching.

Mr. Bell worked for a few days developing a curriculum for an after-school reading and math program that incorporated art, music, and service to and from the community. Mr. Bell planned, upon gaining approval from the administration, that he would offer the program to his current students and to any other interested students in the school. He planned to work throughout the year in developing the summer program during his spare time.

Mr. Bell's ideas for the after-school program involved assistance from community members to teach art and music, including field trips within the community and service-learning projects directed by the students. Mr. Bell would make the necessary connections between the fine arts to literacy and math, with assistance from graduate students from his university. Confident about the potential of the program, Mr. Bell took his ideas to the administration.

Although Mr. Bell was nervous about approaching his administration with the potential of instituting new programs at the school, as a novice teacher, he believed that he had the best interests of the students in mind, and he knew that he had the support of at least one teacher, Mr. Johnson.

When approaching Ms. Rutherford, a ten-year veteran principal, with a five-year tenure at John Dewey, Mr. Bell came prepared. He set up the meeting a week in advance and arrived early, armed with research to support his curricular choices, as well as a detailed outline of the program, including sample lesson plans. He had also provided Ms. Rutherford with these materials a week earlier.

Ms. Rutherford invited Mr. Bell into her office where the two sat down at a conference table. Ms. Rutherford began, "Let me first say how impressed I am with your hard work. I think the program is sound. Unfortunately, we have no money to fund it. I may be able to find you some books, but I can provide no support for staffing, bussing, or anything else."

Excitedly, Mr. Bell replied, "I appreciate your support, but we are not in need of any financial contribution from the school. I have secured partnerships with public libraries in the area and community members who will provide art and music supplies, and we will just piece it together. I know this is not necessarily sustainable, but it is a start. I have also secured graduate students seeking teacher certification to serve as literacy and math tutors for the program, which will count for their field experiences.

These students are also willing and able to conduct research on the effectiveness of the program and on what works, so we will be able to create research-based solutions to the real learning challenges of our students. Everybody wins. Moreover, I have applied for a small federal grant to pay for the background checks for community members working in the school so that the fees will not come from their own pockets, since they are already doing so much for the students and the school."

Ms. Rutherford paused to determine if Mr. Bell had more to say. Upon discerning that he was anxiously awaiting her reply, she spoke, "I admire your passion. But, what about your time? We cannot compensate you for this. We may be able to find funds for summer school stipends, but we cannot pay you throughout the school year for your after-school time."

"I understand that," Mr. Bell replied. "Please understand. This is my community. This is my school. I am willing to go above and beyond to help, and this experience will benefit me as well. I will learn much about how to best to teach our students and how to bridge the divide between the school and the community. This is what we need, and I am willing to do the work. What are our next steps?"

"Again, I can see that you are passionate," Ms. Rutherford explained, "which is exactly what we need at John Dewey. We have not had passion here for some time. I can see the students in your classroom and their parents getting onboard immediately. However, we need more than just your students. In my mind, we need the most at-risk students from all grades invested in your program; the parents as well. If we do not improve as a whole, as a school, we will not survive."

"Agreed." Mr. Bell nodded. "Can I count on your support to this end? And, if so, how do we go about gaining support from everyone else?"

"You have my full support. One hundred percent. As you know, we need to gain the support of the other teachers. If they buy in, and encourage their students and their parents to support this, then we can make great changes. I think we should present your ideas at the next faculty meeting."

Mr. Bell agreed, despite his reservations. He was a brand new teacher. He was not only hesitant at the prospect of speaking in front of his peers, but also at the prospect of attempting to convince veteran teachers and a cadre of substitutes, who most likely would not even attend this meeting, how they needed to change not only their practices, but also their beliefs.

Mr. Bell decided to do some PR before the faculty meeting. He spoke to every single faculty member and substitute teacher in the school, informing them of the program, highlighting the benefits, and the meager involvement that he asked of them: to inspire their students to join and to convince their parents to support the program.

A week later at the faculty meeting, Mr. Bell, with the full support of Ms. Rutherford, shared his program ideas with his colleagues and asked if they would like to offer the program to their own students.

The room was silent, until Ms. Green, a ten-year veteran of the school spoke up, "Our students need help, but this will never work. This program involves students working on their own. The parents will never ensure that they will do their homework, let alone read."

The room was silent. Mr. Bell took the silence to mean quiet acquiescence to Ms. Green's point of view, until Ms. Williams stood and spoke.

"Look," Ms. Williams implored, "I have to acknowledge that I was completely and utterly unprepared for this position. I thought that being educated at one of the best schools in the country would have prepared me for anything, but I was wrong. I am at a loss on how to connect with my students. Duane at least wants to try. Why can't we just give him the benefit of the doubt and support his work? What have we got to lose?"

Mr. Bell smiled and waited. He felt the crowd visibly shift. He could see minds turning and heads nodding. Then, Mr. Johnson stood up. "I want you to know, I still believe in this community. And I believe in Mr. Bell. We have nothing to lose in supporting his proposal and this program. If we do not do this, then we are effectively communicating that we do not believe that our children can learn. If this is what we believe, then none of us should be here."

Given what you know about John Dewey Elementary school, the teacher turnover rate, the needs of the community, and Ms. Rutherford and Mr. Bell, what is the best course of action in this case?

TEACHING NOTES

Selective teacher certification programs like Teach for America prepare their candidates quickly for work in high-poverty or urban communities. Although research indicates that these teachers are successful, most leave the profession after two to three years (Henry, Bastian, & Smith, 2012).

Educators must have knowledge of the needs of students, parents, or caregivers, strategies for collaborating with families and community members, and methods of mobilizing community resources (Anderson, Christenson, & Sinclair, 2004; Epstein & Sanders, 2006; Harris & Chapman, 2002). Having a basic knowledge of the community and cultural competence helps teachers and administrators understand, appreciate, and use the community's diverse cultural, social, and intellectual community resources in support of student needs (Bustamante, Nelson, & Onwuegbuzie, 2009).

Cultural competence refers to the ability of an educator to understand his/her own cultural background and values, and to work successfully with individuals of different cultures without engaging in deficit categorization of them. Given the growing diversity of students, their families, and communities, cultural competence is critical to building a welcoming environment for learning in schools and at home.

This capacity is sometimes referred to as engaging in leadership with cross-cultural skills. School-wide cultural competence can be supported by programs designed to increase understanding and appreciation of cultural differences, as well as commonalities, and serve as the foundation for cultural relationships (Bustamante, Nelson, & Onwuegbuzie, 2009; Evans, 2007).

Rodriguez (2013) defines Funds of Knowledge as an accumulation of historically developed cultural truths, stores of knowledge, and skills that promote the functioning, development, and well-being of individuals and households. Our respective view of the world is based on our store of prior knowledge manifested by cultural events, experiences, and activities, labeled as Funds of Knowledge (Mintzes & Wanderse, 1997; Moll & Greenberg, 1990).

Tapping into students' prior cultural knowledge can help to establish dynamic mental models that network to the learners' existing schema, adding meaning to the new knowledge for the learner (Griner & Stewart, 2012; Moll, Amanti, Neff, & González, 1992). During instruction, this knowledge should be used strategically, encouraged, and applied systematically (Rueda, Monzó, & Higareda, 2004).

According to Cohen (2004), when students are involved in curriculum that reflect their experiences, they will be more secure about learning. "Inquiry does not occur on demand or when teachers are forced to pursue someone else's topic or question. They need time to find the questions that really matter in their lives" (Cohen, 2004, p. 54).

Dewey (1902) advocated for a child-centered approach to writing and discussed the importance of the use of personal perspective in writing. Both are important; both are necessary. Bakhtinian theory suggests that language results from participation in particular contexts and communities (Bakhtin, 1981). Teachers can provide opportunities for students to evolve through prior knowledge and experiences (Driscoll, 1994).

The Funds of Knowledge framework dispels the widely held belief that low-income and non-dominant students do not possess the home knowledge that leads to academic or school success (DaSilva Iddings, Combs, & Moll, 2014). Funds of Knowledge is a revolt against the deficit model of education that funnels non-dominant students into special education or alternative programs with heightened disciplinary structures (Griner & Stewart, 2012; Milner, 2013c).

It encourages questioning of hegemonic teaching and learning traditions in favor of co-creating curriculum and pedagogy utilizing home languages and knowledge by creating "new ways of engaging proactively with critical, voiced involvement at every stage of teaching and learning" (Rodriguez, 2013, p. 108).

According to Ladson-Billings (2009), teachers must study their students in order to decide what and how to teach. Students and teachers should co-construct knowledge by using out-of-school literacies or home knowledge that can be connected to in-school instruction (Milner, 2013a).

ADDITIONAL READING

Reading is Fundamental. (n.d.). *Motivating kids to read: Keeping kids off the summer slide.* http://www.rif.org/us/literacy-resources/articles/keeping-kids-off-the-summer-slide.htm.

Edutopia. (2013, June 4). Resources to prevent summer slide: Virtual field trips, DIY projects and summer reading. http://www.edutopia.org/blog/resources-prevent-summer-slide-matt-davis.

Epstein, J. L., & Sanders, M. G. (2006). Prospects for change: Preparing educators for school, family, and community partnerships. *Peabody Journal of Education, 81*(2), 81–120.

Evans, A. E. (2007). School leaders and their sensemaking about race and demographic change. *Educational Administration Quarterly, 43*(2), 159–88.

Harris, A., & Chapman, C. (2002). *Effective leadership in schools facing challenging circumstances.* London: National College for School Leadership.

National Council of Teachers of English. (2015). *Readwritethink.* http://www.readwritethink.org/search/?resource_type_filtering=70-7274768082113&resource_type=70&sort_order=alpha&q=Writing&srchgo.x=0&srchgo.y=0&old_q=&srchwhere=par.

Colorado, C. (2010). *Summer learning resources for parents.* http://www.colorincolorado.org/article/24695/.

QUESTIONS FOR DISCUSSION

1. What challenges do you foresee Mr. Bell experiencing as he attempts to change this school culture?
2. Why do you think Ms. Williams was assigned Mr. Bell as her mentee?
3. Why did it take Ms. Williams, a white woman who was unfamiliar with the community, for the teachers at John Dewey to listen to Mr. Bell's proposal?
4. What does privilege have to do with this case?
5. What are the potential problems underlying these students' needs, interests, and potential struggles?
6. What can be done to inspire literacy engagement?
7. How will community partnerships help support student achievement? You have many students in your class or school who are "resistant readers," or subject to the summer slide. What strategies will you devise or support?

ADDITIONAL ACTIVITIES

In small groups, discuss the types of data that you would collect if you were a staff member at John Dewey assessing the effectiveness of the after-school program. How might you use these data and subsequent analysis to create feedback for improving instruction and student engagement? (See Halverson, 2010.)

Further, how can the data be used as evidence to facilitate understandings that strengthen relationships between the school and the community? Descriptive literature (Epstein et al., 2002; Landsman, 2006) has offered strategies for collection of evidence through regular phone calls to parents, neighborhood bus tours, and home visits.

REFERENCES

Anderson, A. R., Christenson, S. L., & Sinclair, M. F. (2004). Check & connect: The importance of relationships for promoting engagement with school. *Journal of School Psychology*, *42*(2), 95–113.

Bakhtin, M. M. (1981). *The dialogic imagination: Four essays*. Austin, TX: The University of Texas Press.

Bustamante, R. M., Nelson, J. A., & Onwuegbuzie, A. J. (2009). Assessing school wide cultural competence: Implications for school leadership preparation. *Educational Administration Quarterly*, *45*(5), 793–827.

Carter, P. L., & Welner, K. G. (Eds.). (2013). *Closing the opportunity gap: What America must do to give every child an even change*. New York, NY: Oxford University Press.

Charity Hudley, A. H., & Mallinson, C. (2011). *Understanding English language variation in U.S. schools*. New York, NY: Teachers College Press.

Cohen, B. (2004). The zine project: Writing with a personal perspective. *Language Arts*, 82, 129-138.

Darling Hammond, L. (2010). *The flat world and education: How America's commitment to equity will determine our future*. New York, NY: Teachers College Press.

DaSilva Iddings, A. C., Combs, M. C., & Moll, L. C. (2014). English language learners and partnerships with families, communities, teacher preparation, and schools. In H. R. Milner & K. Lomotey (Eds.), *Handbook of urban education* (pp. 188–96). New York, NY: Routledge.

Delpit, L. (1988). The silenced dialogue: Pedagogy and power in educating other people's children. *Harvard Educational Review*, *58*, 280–98.

Delpit, L. (2009). Language diversity and learning. In A. Darder, M. P. Baltodano, & R. D. Torres (Eds.), *The critical pedagogy reader* (2nd ed.) (pp. 325–37). New York, NY: Routledge.

Dewey, J. (1902). *The child and the curriculum*. Chicago: University of Chicago Press.

Driscoll, M. (1994). *Psychology of learning for instruction*. Boston, MA: Allyn and Bacon.

Epstein, J. L., & Sanders, M. G. (2006). Prospects for change: Preparing educators for school, family, and community partnerships. *Peabody Journal of Education*, *81*(2), 81–120.

Evans, A. E. (2007). School leaders and their sensemaking about race and demographic change. *Educational Administration Quarterly*, *43*(2), 159–88.

Freire, P. (1970) *Pedagogy of the oppressed*. New York, NY: The Continuum Publishing Company.

Freire, P. (1985). *The politics of education: Culture, power and liberation*. New York, NY: Bergin & Garvey.

Goldenberg, B. (2014). White teachers in urban classrooms embracing non-white students' cultural capital for better teaching and learning. *Urban Education, 49*(1), 111–44.

Goff, P. A., Jackson, M. C., Di Leone, B. A. L., Culotta, C. M., & DiTomasso, N. A. (2014, February). The essence of innocence: Consequences of dehumanizing black children. *Journal of Personality and Social Psychology.* http://www.apa.org/pubs/journals/releases/psp-a0035663.pdf.

Griner, A. C., & Stewart, M. L. (2012). Addressing the achievement gap and disproportionality through the use of culturally responsive teaching practices. *Urban Education, 48*(4), 585–621.

Haddix, M., & Price-Dennis, D. (2013). Urban fiction and multicultural literature as transformative tools for preparing English teachers for diverse classrooms. *English Education, 45*(3), 247–83.

Harris, A., & Chapman, C. (2002). *Effective leadership in schools facing challenging circumstances.* London: National College for School Leadership.

Henry, G. T., Bastian, K. C., & Smith, A. A. (2012). Scholarships to recruit the "best and brightest" into teaching: Who is recruited, where do they teach, how effective are they, and how long do they stay? *Educational Researcher, 41*(3), 83–92.

Howard, T. C., & Milner, H. R. (2014). Teacher preparation for urban schools. In H. R. Milner & K. Lomotey (Eds.), *Handbook of urban education* (pp. 199–216). New York, NY: Routledge.

Kohl, H. (1994). *I won't learn from you and other thoughts on creative maladjustment.* New York, NY: The New Press.

Kozol, J. (2005). *The shame of the nation: The restoration of apartheid schooling in America.* New York, NY: Crown.

Ladson-Billings, G. (2009). *The dreamkeepers: Successful teachers of African American children* (2nd ed.). San Francisco, CA: Jossey-Bass.

Landsman, J. (2009). *A white teacher talks about race.* Lanham, MD: Rowman & Littlefield Publishers, Inc.

Macedo, D. (2006). *Literacies of power: What Americans are not allowed to know with new commentary by Shirley Steinberg, Joe Kincheloe, and Peter McLaren.* Boulder, CO: Westview Press.

Milner, H. R. (2013a). Analyzing poverty, learning, and teaching through a critical race theory lens. *Review of Research in Education, 37*, 1–53.

Milner, H. R. (2013b). *Start where you are, but don't stay there: Understanding diversity, opportunity gaps, and teaching in today's classrooms.* Cambridge, MA: Harvard Education Press.

Milner, H. R. (2013c). Why are students of color (still) punished more severely than and frequently than white students? *Urban Education, 48*(4), 483–89.

Milner, H. R., & Lomotey, K. (Eds.). (2014). *Handbook of urban education.* New York, NY: Routledge.

Mintzes, J., & Wanderse, J. H. (1997). Reform and innovation in science teaching: A human constructivist view. In J. J. Mintzes, J. H. Wandersee, & J. D. Novak (Eds.), *Teaching science for understanding: A human constructivist view* (pp. 29–58). San Diego, CA: Academic Press.

Moje, E. B. (1999). From expression to dialogue: A study of social action literacy projects in an urban school setting. *The Urban Review, 31*(3), 305–30.

Moll, L.C., & Greenberg, J.B. (1990). Creating zones of possibilites: Combining social contexts for instruction. In L.C. Moll (Ed.), Vygotsky and education (pp.319-348). Cambridge, MA: Cambridge University Press.

Moll, L. C., Amanti, D., Neff, D., & González, N. (1992). Funds of knowledge for teaching. *Theory Into Practice, 31*, 132–41.

Nilep, C. (2006, June). "Code switching" in sociocultural linguistics. *Colorado Research in Linguistics, 19*, 1–22.

Phuntsog, N. (2001, April). Culturally responsive teaching: What do selected United States elementary school teachers think? *Intercultural Education, 12*(1), 51–64.

Reading is Fundamental. (n.d.). *Motivating kids to read: Keeping kids off the summer slide.* http://www.rif.org/us/literacy-resources/articles/keeping-kids-off-the-summer-slide.htm.

Rodriguez, G. M. (2013). Power and agency in education: Exploring the pedagogical dimensions of funds of knowledge. *Review of Research in Education, 37*, 87–120.

Rueda, R., Monzó, L. D., & Higareda, I. (2004). Appropriating the sociocultural resources of latino paraeducators for effective instruction with latino students. *Urban Education, 39*(1), 52–90.

Salazar, M. (2013). A humanizing pedagogy: Reinventing the principles and practice of education as a journey toward liberation. *Review of Research in Education, 37*, 121–48.

Uhlenberg, J., & Brown, K. M. (2002). Racial gap in teachers' perceptions of the achievement gap. *Urban Education, 34*(4), 493–530.

Weis, L., & Fine, M. (Eds.). (2005). *Beyond silenced voices: Class, race, and gender in United States schools.* Albany, NY: State University of New York Press.

White, J. W. (2011). De-centering English: Highlighting the dynamic nature of the English language to promote the teaching of code-switching. *English Journal, 100*(4), 44–49.

Chapter Eight

Marginalization or Necessary Push-Out?

Educating ELL Students

INTRODUCTION

The policies and legal issues raised in this case include English Only movements, the education of immigrant and ethnic student populations, the Third-Grade Reading Guarantee, and the banning of Ethnic Studies courses and programs in Arizona.

The banning of Ethnic Studies programs began in Arizona in 2010, which exacerbated the already contentious political climate in schools. Deemed to be anti-American by various right-wing politicians, although contributing to the general well-being and graduation rates of ethnic minorities in Arizona schools, such courses and programs were banned in 2010. This legislation contributes to the alienation of various minority groups in the state. A foundational text in the field of education, *Pedagogy of the Oppressed* by Paulo Freire (1970), was among the books banned.

This case centers on Noemi, a recent immigrant to Arizona and English Language Learner (ELL). Two laws impact Noemi: English-only and the Third-Grade Reading Guarantee. The law states that students falling far below grade level on the third-grade reading assessment will not be promoted to the third grade, with two exceptions: one, the student is an ELL or is deemed Limited English Proficient, receiving less than two years of English instruction; or, two, is a student possessing a disability and possesses an individualized education plan (IEP).

8

90 *Chapter 8*

Although Noemi is primarily Spanish speaking, the district policy of English Only requires her primary subjects be taught only in English. Additionally, if Noemi does not show that she is reading at a third-grade level in English by the end of the year, she will be retained. This case asks the reader to reflect on the laws and policies that impact children, and to make determinations about how to best meet the interests of the child depicted in this case in light of or in spite of these provisions.

THE CASE

> English language learners are the fastest-growing student population group in our schools. Providing them with high-quality services and programs is an important investment in America's future.
> –National Education Association President Dennis Van Roekel

Noemi recently emigrated from a rural area in Honduras to Arizona and is an ELL. Although approximately 83 percent of the population in Honduras is literate, with bilingual (Spanish/English) and even trilingual (Spanish/English/Arabic or Spanish/English/German) schools, the rural populations lack access to consistent schooling. The primary school completion rate is reported to be approximately 40 percent.

Arriving in the United States in May, Noemi had been in the country for five months prior to entering Jane Addams Elementary for third grade. She had little experience with English literacy prior to entering the United States. Arizona has two laws impacting Noemi: English-only and the Third-Grade Reading Guarantee.

In general, ELL students are more likely to stay in school if they feel connected to their teachers (Catterall, 1998; De La Cruz, 2008; Englund, Egeland, & Collins, 2008). Teachers who provide extra attention and support can be transformational in the education and retention of ELL students. Teachers of ELL students who understand the importance of getting to know their students and their cultures can have a lasting impact.

Definitions

ELL Students

According to No Child Left Behind (NCLB) (2002):

> NCLB uses the term Limited English Proficient (LEP) and defines an ELL student as an individual who (a) is age [three to twenty-one] years; (b) is enrolled or preparing to enroll in elementary or secondary school; (c) was not born in the U.S. or whose native language is not English; (d) is a Native American, Alaskan Native, or a resident of outlying areas; (e) comes from an

environment in which a language other than English has had a significant impact on an individual's ELP; (f) is migratory and comes from an environment where English is not the dominant language; and (g) has difficulties in speaking, reading, writing, or understanding the English language that may deny the individual the ability to meet the state's proficient level of achievement, to successfully achieve in classrooms where English is the language of instruction, or to participate fully in society. (NCLB, 2002, n.p.)

Third-Grade Reading Guarantee in Arizona

Arizona law requires that students falling far below grade level on the third-grade reading assessment will not be promoted to the third grade, with two exceptions: one, the student is an ELL or is deemed Limited English Proficient, receiving less than two years of English instruction; or, two, the student possesses a disability and an IEP, and the IEP team has decided, along with the parent or guardian that promotion is appropriate and in accordance with the IEP (Arizona Revised Statute 15-701).

Starting in 2013/2014, every third-grade student in Arizona must demonstrate proficiency in reading; otherwise, they are not allowed to advance to the fourth grade. House Bill 2732, the high-stakes reading mandate, was modeled after a 2002 Florida law.

English Only

English Only is a movement that began in California in the late 1990s, arguing that traditional bilingual programs prevented immigrants from readily learning English and from valuing English as the primary spoken language.

English Only laws, including Proposition 227 (State of California, 1998), advocate against bilingual programs and link the poor academic performance of non-English speakers, most of whom are Spanish speakers, to their placement in bilingual education programs. This legislation sought to make English Only programs the standard education for ELL students. The first English Only law was passed in 1998.

ELL Teachers

The majority of general education teachers have little to no training in teaching ELL students (Hopkins, Lowenhaupt, & Sweet, 2015). Because teaching English as a second language is not considered to be an academic discipline, teachers of ELL students often find their expertise questioned or undervalued. This can lead to ELL student needs being unattended in general education classrooms (Hopkins, Lowenhaupt, & Sweet, 2015, p. 412).

Push-Out

English as a Second Language programs have traditionally utilized pullout programs, which remove ELL students from their regular classroom for an allotted period of time in order to provide these students with explicit language instruction in English. Conversely, push-in and co-teaching models require teachers of ELL students and general education teachers to work in collaboration (Hopkins, Lowenhaupt, & Sweet, 2015, p. 411).

The classification of ELL students as "English learner" to "fluent English proficient" is important, but not without controversy. When a student is deemed "fluent English proficient," the student is able to enter the educational mainstream. However, this reclassification has lasting implications for students.

According to Umansky and Reardon (2014),

> English learner status is designed to support students learning English with specially prepared teachers, content instruction taught with modifications to increase English learner accessibility, English language development classes, and regular monitoring and English language proficiency assessments. Once reclassified, students lose access to these specialized services but gain access to mainstream classes including the full breath of courses, teachers, and peers. (p. 880)

Arizona promotes reclassification after one year (Umansky & Reardon, 2014). However, research suggests that reclassification can take between four to ten years, and is slower for students living in or coming from poverty (Umansky & Reardon, 2014).

A National Problem

According to the National Education Association (NEA; 2008),

> Teachers lack practical, research-based information, resources, and strategies needed to teach, evaluate, and nurture ELL students, whether those students were born in this country or elsewhere, or whether they are the first, second, or third generation to attend an American public school. In too many cases, ELL students are being given reading and math tests in English before they are proficient in the language. (p. 1–2)

The academic performance of ELL students is well below that of their peers. ELL students also have an excessively high dropout rate (NEA, 2008). In the 2005 National Assessment of Educational Progress, 29 percent of ELLs scored at or above the basic level in reading, compared with 75 percentof their peers (NEA, 2008).

Additional Political Battles in Arizona

In addition to the English Only movements, recent political battles in Arizona impact the education of immigrant and ethnic student populations, most notably the banning of Ethnic Studies courses and programs. The banning of Ethnic Studies programs began in 2010, which has exacerbated the political climate in schools.

For example, Noemi, mentioned earlier in the chapter, is primarily Spanish speaking, the district policy of English Only, or English Immersion, permits her primary subjects be taught only in English. Additionally, if Noemi does not show that she is reading at a third-grade level in English by the end of the year, she will be retained.

Noemi has four hours of ELL instruction throughout each school day, but her core subjects—math, social studies, reading, and science—are all taught in English. Although Noemi was considered to be academically talented in her home country, despite her disparate instruction, her current teacher for her primary subjects as well as her peers perceive her to be less than average.

Some teachers view ELL students as similar to low-performing English-speaking students leading to watered-down curriculums, including delivering reading instruction with materials well below the students' comprehension levels. These curricular and cultural mismatches contribute to the low academic performance levels of many ELL students (Coyne, Kami'enui, & Carnine, 2010).

Because the United States is primarily a monolingual country, students and teachers often cannot see beyond language barriers. Noemi's teacher for her core subjects, Ms. Sanders, has little to no exposure to any language other than English. A recent transfer to the building, she also has had little exposure to ELL students.

Research indicates that novice teachers are more likely to be placed in ELL content-based courses (Blanca Dabach, 2015). According to Blanca Dabach (2015), "Low student status also became associated with teacher status within schools, and lack of teaching experience justified placing teachers with less experience into lower-track classes" (p. 248).

Noemi is a happy child and has made a few English-speaking friends in her primary subjects, despite the language barrier. However, Noemi is teased by her some of peers and taunted that she should "speak English." Her teacher, Ms. Sanders, does nothing to correct this behavior.

A common mistake with some teachers is assuming that ELL students are not intelligent because they may not participate or speak up in class. Many teachers are afraid to approach ELL students and do not take the opportunity to get to know them. Ms. Sanders is guilty of both of these mindsets.

She placed Noemi's desk at the rear of the classroom and diverts her attention from her. Noemi smiles at Ms. Sanders each morning as she enters the classroom and greets her with "Hola Señora Sanders." Ms. Sanders has never responded to Noemi's greetings, nor has she attempted to learn even rudimentary Spanish in order to communicate with or assist Noemi.

Because her school does not have enough ELL students to justify an entire class of same aged peers (or similarly proficient English-speaking students), Noemi is in an ELL class with students in various grades and English proficiency levels ranging from kindergarten to sixth grade.

Because of this large range, the one ELL teacher in the building, Ms. Weller, struggles to meet all of her students' needs. Ms. Weller, a native English speaker, double majored in Spanish and Early Childhood Education as an undergraduate, but had not used her Spanish in several years before being hired from within her district to direct the ELL program at Jane Addams Elementary.

Although not specifically trained to work with ELL students, Ms. Weller is committed to her students. When her Spanish fails her, she relies on Google Translator to help with her Spanish literacy and in sending notes home to parents with homework and suggestions on how parents can assist their children. Ms. Weller knows that she needs help in assisting these students.

In addition to taking free Spanish courses at her local community center in the evenings, she is also in the process of pursuing an ELL certification at her own expense. Although she has asked that the district reimburse her for her university fees, the district has declined her request.

Ms. Weller also attempts to communicate with parents through home visits to better meet the needs of her students. Upon her first visit to Noemi's home, Ms. Weller learned that Noemi felt very strange upon entering Jane Addams Elementary because she did not understand anything that was going on around her. She felt singled out.

She confided in Ms. Weller that she was often the target of teasing by her peers and often felt that her peers were talking about her. She also admitted that she believed her teacher, Ms. Sanders, witnessed some of this behavior but failed to do anything to protect her. Noemi's parents expressed shock at these sentiments, for Noemi had never communicated these issues to them. Ms. Weller was comforted by the fact that Noemi had supportive parents: upon hearing of Noemi's struggles, her parents rushed to her side to provide hugs and words of assurance and support.

Upon subsequent home visits, Ms. Weller learned that Noemi felt that her parents were the most influential factors in her educational motivation and success; she desired to please them, for their primary reason for immigrating to the United States was so that Noemi could receive a good education. They felt this likely would not happen in their small rural village in Honduras.

Parental expectations and family relationships can shape student's perseverance and achievement in school (De La Cruz, 2008; Englund, Egeland, &

Collins, 2008). Noemi's parents stressed homework completion and the importance of education, to which both Noemi was committed (Fulgini, 1997).

After several home visits, and Ms. Weller's unrelenting attempts to communicate with the family despite her own language barriers, both Noemi and her family began to trust Ms. Weller. Eventually, Ms. Weller learned of the failure of Ms. Sanders to communicate with Noemi. Noemi's tearful confession of her invisibility in Ms. Sander's class also left Ms. Weller in tears.

Upon Ms. Weller's return to school the next day, she knew she had to speak to Ms. Sanders to determine the best course of action. She saw Ms. Sanders as she walked from the parking lot into the school. "Excuse me, Ms. Sanders?"

"Yes?" Ms. Sanders replied.

"I would like to speak to you about a student in your class, Noemi?"

Ms. Sanders rolled her eyes. "What about her?"

"Well," Ms. Weller began, "I have visited the home several times, and I understand that the family wants the best for Noemi. They help her every night as best they can, and I was just wondering . . ."

Ms. Sanders cut her off, "I know you are just doing your job, but this student probably will not be here for long and because I cannot educate the parents, I cannot do much for her. Likely, she will be deported soon. I have twenty-five other students that I need to focus on. I do not have time for this. I have to get to class." And with that, Ms. Sanders rushed into the school.

Ms. Weller realized that she would be wasting her time trying to change the mind of Ms. Sanders on anything relating to Noemi from this point forward, but she was troubled by Ms. Sanders's assumption that Noemi and her family were undocumented. She wondered if she should report this conversation to her administrator.

As a new teacher, she was fearful of approaching her administrator with problems. Already overwhelmed with a large population of ELL students and other staff problems, the administrator maintained neither an open door policy for faculty nor any mentoring programs for new teachers.

Ms. Weller knew from her ELL certification program that teachers with no training in the area of ELL language development may create instructional and pedagogical styles largely governed by stereotypes, which she felt would likely be exacerbated by the current political climate of the contentious issue of the banning of ethic studies in the state.

Ms. Weller knew that she would need to focus on institutional factors impacting Noemi and her family. However, Ms. Sanders's evaluation of Noemi would impact her potential retention or her continued educational progression at Jane Addams.

Another major problem that Ms. Weller saw in her district was a direct result of English Only policies. There were few books and instructional materials written in Spanish in the school, or written in both English and

Spanish. Most books were written in English. The policy governing the district reads as follows, "Although teachers may use a minimal amount of the child's native language when necessary, no subject matter shall be taught in any language other than English, and children in this program learn to read and write solely in English" (English-Only vs. English-Only, 2000, n.p.).

With a relative lack of support from her district, Ms. Weller struggles, particularly in the current contentious political climate of how to best serve her students.

ADDITIONAL RESOURCES

American Psychological Association. (2015). *The English-only movement.* http://www.apa.org/pi/oema/resources/english-only.aspx.

The Arizona Republic. (2010, September 4). *New Arizona law: Future 3rd-graders to have to read to pass grade.* http://archive.azcentral.com/arizonarepublic/local/articles/20100904arizona-3rd-graders-must-pass-reading.html#ixzz3ei8ZlcrB.

Ballotpedia. (2006). *Arizona English as the official language, Proposition 103.* http://ballotpedia.org/Arizona_English_as_the_Official_Language,_Proposition_103_%282006%29.

Hamayan, E. V. (2012). Education policy and our perception of ELL performance. *Colorin Colorado.* http://www.colorincolorado.org/article/50359/.

The Huffington Post. (2015, July 2). *Arizona ethnic studies ban.* http://www.huffingtonpost.com/news/arizona-ethnic-studies-ban/.

N. A. (2014, December). *Structured English immersion models of the Arizona English language learners task force.* http://www.azed.gov/english-language-learners/files/2015/01/structured-english-immersion-models-revised-december-2014.pdf.

Speaking in tongues: Four kids, four languages, one city, one world. (n.d.). How 'submersion' differs from immersion. http://speakingintonguesfilm.info/brain/how-submersion-differs-from-immersion/.

Youtube. (2011). Arizona's attack on Ethnic Studies in Tucson. https://www.youtube.com/watch?v=76Y0Z8NmHyY.

Youtube. (2010). Lawsuit filed against Arizona ethnic studies ban. https://www.youtube.com/watch?v=o-a2q3MqMOQ.

Wright, W. E. (2012). Beware of the VAM: Valued-added measures for teacher accountability. *Colorin Colorado.* http://www.colorincolorado.org/article/50576/.

QUESTIONS FOR DISCUSSION

1. Whose political interests do the policies implied in this case serve?
2. If Noemi just entered your school, how would you help her?
3. What messages are being sent to and about ELL students within this school?
4. What can the school community do about this? What should be done?
5. What are the philosophical debates in this case?
6. Are English Only policies ethical? Do they represent best practice for the equitable education of our children?
7. What are this student's learning needs and how may the school address them?

8. What could Ms. Weller do to better address Noemi's needs?
9. How could the community be brought into the school to assist in this situation?
10. How should teachers and administration advocate for students like Noemi?
11. How could professional development and teacher collaboration assist with this case?
12. Ultimately, what should Ms. Weller do?

ADDITIONAL ACTIVITIES

1. After reading the additional resources, what is your opinion of English Only or English Immersion as opposed to bilingual education? Whose interests are served by these positions? Which positions would you advocate for in your school or district and why?
2. According to Critical Race Theory (Chapman, 2007), majoritarian discourses must be interrogated and social, political, and educational issues examined through the prioritization of student voices. The notions of "good student" and "involved parent" must be re-examined. Scholars of Critical Race Theory seek to dismantle of the stereotypes of non-dominant students by investigating their unique experiences with school. According to Chapman, "The focus on deficit notions of students of color and the simplification of classroom complexity does very little to empower teachers and students" (2007, p. 161). How does this theory apply to this case?
3. Investigate English Only policies and the banning of Ethnic Studies in Arizona. How do these laws affect immigrant and ELL students and the teachers who teach them?
4. The NEA advocates for the following changes to NCLB in order to assist ELL students: the extension from one year to a maximum of three years in the time for an ELL student to master the language before being tested in core content areas; the improvement of the quality of assessments for ELL students (including native language tests); the assurance that all ELL students will be provided the full range of services they need in order to bring them to English proficiency and to improve their performance in academic content areas; and the improvement of teacher training programs and development so teachers can better meet the needs of ELL students (p. 3). Do you agree with the NEA policy proscriptions? Explain your answer.

REFERENCES

Arizona Revised Statute 15-701. (n.d.). http://www.azleg.gov/ars/15/00701.htm.

Blanca Dabach, D. (2015). Teacher placement into immigrant English learner classrooms: Limiting access in comprehensive high schools. *American Educational Research Journal*, *52*(2), 243–74.

Catterall, J. S. (Feb., 1998). Risk and resilience in student transition to high school. *American Journal of Education*, *106*(2), 302–33.

Coyne, M. D., Kami'enui, E. J., & Carnine, D. W. (2010, July 20). Problems in current instruction of English language learners. *Education.com*. http://www.education.com/reference/article/problems-instruction-english-learners/.

De La Cruz, Y. (Jan., 2008). Who mentors Hispanic ELLs? *Journal of Hispanic Higher Education*, *7*(1), 31–42.

English-Only vs. English-Only. (2000). A tale of two initiatives: California and Arizona. http://www.languagepolicy.net/archives/203-227.htm.

Englund, M. M., Egeland, B., & Collins, W. A. (2008). Exceptions to high school dropout predictions in a low income sample: Do adults make a difference? *Journal of Social Issues*, *64*(1), 77–93.

Freire, P. (1970). *Pedagogy of the oppressed*. New York, NY: Bloomsbury.

Andrew J. Fuligni, A. J. (1997). The academic achievement of adolescents from immigrant families: The role of family background, attitudes, and behavior. *Child Development*, 68(2), 351–363.

Hopkins, M., Lowenhaupt, R., & Sweet, T. M. (2015). Organizing English leaner instruction in new immigrant destinations: District infrastructure and subject-specific school practice. *American Educational Research Journal*, *52*(3), 408–39.

No Child Left Behind. (2002). No child left behind: A desktop reference. https://www2.ed.gov/admins/lead/account/nclbreference/reference.pdf.

National Education Association. (2008). Policy brief: English language learners face unique challenges. http://www.nea.org/assets/docs/HE/ELL_Policy_Brief_Fall_08_%282%29.pdf.

Need to know on PBS. (2013, February). *Explore the banned curriculum*. http://www.pbs.org/wnet/need-to-know/culture/explore-the-banned-curriculum/16309/oppressed.

Research and Development. (n.d.). Redesign education. http://blog.researchdevelop.org/post/32885774152/suppressing-the-pedagogy-of-the-oppressed.

State of California. (1998, June 2). Proposition 227: English language in public schools. http://www.smartvoter.org/1998jun/ca/state/prop/227/.

Umansky, I. M., & Reardon, S. F. (2014). Reclassification patterns among Latino English learner students in bilingual, dual immersion, and English immersion classrooms. *American Educational Research Journal*, *51*(5), 879–912.

Chapter Nine

Sex Discrimination at University X

INTRODUCTION

Gender inequity remains a problem in all areas of education. Gender inequity tends to occur most often as a result of adherence to the philosophy of essentialism, or the notion that there are fixed characteristics women and men possess, which influences what it means to be feminine or masculine. This philosophy perpetuates the idea that the traditionally held ideas of women as more nurturing and men as more aggressive are natural.

Gender bias occurs when one's expectations and potentialities are limited because of the expectations others place on them and/or upon members of their sex in general, and/or when a person makes assumptions about another person's behavior, preferences, or abilities based only on their gender.

This case asks readers to determine whether sex discrimination has occurred at an institution of higher learning (see Title IX). Dominique, a character in the case, is a strong woman who advocates for herself. Assertive behavior in women is often viewed as disruptive and viewed negatively, especially by those adhering to essentialist mindsets; this provides additional layers to the case. Dominique is also a woman possessing multiple minority statuses, which provides material for additional discussions of intersectionality, which were examined in previous cases.

Additionally, this case describes the experience of Dominique, a new faculty member at University X, as she discovers a wide range of ethical and management problems in her department. The case unfolds as we track her efforts to deal with these issues. Intertwined throughout the case are challenges pertaining to the dean's responsibilities, particularly in the area of management oversight. Students should analyze the case, identify the inconsistencies in ethical behavior, and identify the potential moral and legal consequences.

THE CASE

University X is located in a small midwestern town, and, although many of the students come from rural areas, it is considered urban because of the racial and socio-economic demographics of the city in which it is located. Diversity is promoted among the student body, faculty, staff, and in the interdisciplinary nature of its educational programs. The university is socially involved and addresses urban issues through education, research, and outreach.

The city has more than eighty thousand residents with a racial makeup of 75 percent white, 21 percent African American, 3 percent biracial, and 1 percent other (U.S. Census Bureau, 2010). The median income is $28,730 with approximately 19.2 percent of the population living below the poverty line. The city's economy is primarily industrial; a significant portion of the city's economy is agricultural. However, employment in the area of manufacturing remains in a state of decline.

In 1858, University X was chartered and incorporated having previously functioned as a private academy. In the late nineteenth and early twentieth centuries, University X underwent significant change. The college curriculum was modernized to reflect a liberal arts tradition, and the campus was renovated with new buildings. In keeping with the liberal arts tradition, University X currently offers sixty majors and fifty-three minors of academic coursework. In addition, in 2010 four graduate programs were added to its educational offerings: a Master of Arts in Educational Leadership, a Master of Science in Physician's Assistant, an Educational Specialist in School Psychology, and a doctoral program in Physical Therapy.

From the beginning, University X emphasized Christian teachings as a component of its curriculum and was one of the early coeducational institutions in the United States. The school has approximately two thousand undergraduate students and five hundred graduate students. The institution is considered to be a predominantly white institution with 82 percent of the student population identifying as white.

The students are comprised of 50 percent men and 50 percent women. The school was founded as a place where men and women could be educated with equal opportunity and where there would be no distinction based on race, color, sex, or position. Purposefully, the school attempted to safeguard the values of democracy, equity, diversity, and social justice for students, staff, and faculty.

The education department is housed in one university building and includes a graduate program in educational leadership and general undergraduate education programs, which include intervention specialist, early childhood and middle childhood majors, and an adolescent young adult minor focusing on various licensure areas: math, English, science, foreign language, and social studies.

The faculty is 87.5 percent white. There are a total of eight faculty members, with two men and six women. The male faculty is comprised of 50 percent tenured faculty, while 83.33 percent of the female faculty is untenured.

The Department of Education at University X has one male tenured faculty member and one female tenured faculty member. Both tenured faculty members have been practitioners, one as teacher, and one, Franklin, as teacher, principal, and eventually superintendent. These tenured faculty members do not consider themselves scholars. They are not published in academic presses or peer-reviewed journals.

In addition, there are three untenured female tenure track faculty members in the Department of Education, two of whom are alumni. The third, Dominique, moved from a large metropolitan area to take the tenure track job at University X. Dominique has published several books and has an active record of publishing in peer-reviewed journals. She is the most widely published faculty member in the department. The other two untenured women in the department have no publications.

University X has historically been considered a teaching institution. Student evaluations are the primary consideration for tenure. However, with the recent growth in student enrollment, the addition of graduate programs, and the transition of the institution from a college to a university, there is a new expectation for faculty to conduct research and to publish.

Additionally, there are several adjunct professors, former practitioners, who teach various courses in the Department of Education, as well as a clinical faculty member who serves as the field placement coordinator and teaches in both the undergraduate and graduate programs. There is one departmental assistant as well as a data analyst; both of these administrative staff positions are filled by women.

The faculty members in the Department of Education are largely collegial and congenial with one another, with one exception. Most faculty members are leery of Franklin, the chair of the department who has been the chair for more than fifteen years. In 2010, it was Franklin who was largely responsible for the expansion of program offerings.

Franklin's leadership style is hierarchical. He does not share the budget. He does not participate in departmental tasks that he deems "housekeeping," such as accreditation, departmental reports, or mentoring new faculty. When the dean of the university communicated to him that the Department of

Education should have subcommittees, he created the subcommittees he deemed appropriate and then slotted in those individuals he felt best suited those committees. There was no collaboration, discussion, or choice for the members of the department.

The culture of the department could be defined as a "culture of niceness." Pittard and Butler (2008), define the "culture of niceness" as:

> school culture (including external factors such as school structure, community culture and nature of the profession in general) characterized by conformity and professional interactions wherein the expectation for teachers is to not be confrontational or critical of the school structure, but to accept it or at the very least to work within it without outward resistance. In other words, the expectation is for teachers to "play nice" within the system of schooling, accepting the status quo and modeling it for their students. We see this as part of the "hidden curriculum" of schools and, as such, it is pervasive and invisible at times. (p. 72)

To wit, in this department, questions are perceived as challenges or as confrontations; they are always viewed negatively. If department members are not pulling their weight, someone else, typically the untenured faculty or staff members, "pick up the slack."

Every organization depends on leadership to shape a culture that in many ways is a direct reflection of that leader. Leadership is comprised of the daily actions of a leader, the interactions with those around them, and the relationships that are formed. These leaders recognize faculty as equal partners, acknowledging their professionalism and capitalizing on their knowledge, expertise, and skills (Darling-Hammond, 1988).

Effective leadership involves strategies such as reflective practice, shared decision making, collaboration, and vision building that reflect the values and goals of the organization and the context in which they exist but above all a leader must be honest, fair, trustworthy, transparent, and ethical. Ethical leadership is important in sustaining organizational and personal integrity that shapes a community committed to truthful operations and personal interactions with others.

Characters

Franklin is a full professor at University X. He is both chair of the Department of Education and the program director of the new master's in educational leadership program. He has been a teacher, a principal, and a superintendent on the east coast before coming to University X approximately twenty years prior.

An administrator, Franklin does not publish, but he does attend practitioner conferences. In his twenty years at University X, Franklin has never been elected to a campus committee. He is the only member of the department who has never been elected to a campus committee. This fact is considered among the department to be indicative of his poor reputation on campus. Franklin teaches courses in community engagement and professional development.

Franklin does not run department meetings. Instead, he has allowed Susan, an untenured faculty member and the accreditation coordinator, to call and run all the meetings. Franklin has adopted the practice of hiring his former undergraduate students as professors in the department. As former students, they are grateful to Franklin for having been hired and are also thus hesitant to question or challenge him when asked to complete additional work.

Susan is a young (thirty-five), white, untenured female faculty member working in both the undergraduate and graduate programs at University X (terminal degree holding). She is an alumna of University X and one of Franklin's former students. Susan feels that Franklin has provided her opportunities within the department and is grateful for his help.

Sara is also an alumna and former student of Franklin. Sara is a young (thirty-three), white, untenured female faculty member working in both the undergraduate and graduate programs at University X (terminal degree holding).

Judith is a white, tenured female faculty member in her late forties, working in both the undergraduate and graduate programs at University X (terminal degree holding). She also is the field placement coordinator and hires and evaluates those individuals who supervise student teachers.

David is a white retired schoolteacher, hired by University X's Department of Education to supervise and assess student teachers. He is sixty-two and holds a master's degree in education. Although well liked, Judith desires not to renew David's contract as a supervisor because he does not fulfill all of the expectations for his position. For example, he is unwilling to learn the technology necessary to communicate with student teachers and cooperating teachers working in the schools.

He is also not critical of the students he supervises, providing them with little to no feedback for their own practice and improvement. Judith, as field placement coordinator, has the power not to renew David's employment.

Dominique is a young (thirty-five), African American, untenured female faculty member working in both the undergraduate and graduate programs at University X (terminal degree holding). She hails from a large metropolitan city. Dominique moved to University X to take the tenure track position in the new Master in Educational Leadership program.

She worked for seventeen years in an urban high school teaching English, while also teaching both courses in multicultural education and leadership part-time. Her research interests include educational equity and teaching for social justice. She teaches in both the graduate and undergraduate programs at University X. Dominique has been teaching at University X for two years. In her first year, she was elected to the university's diversity committee. In her second year, she won two campus diversity awards and was elected to chair the diversity committee.

Marcia is a white administrative assistant in the department of education at University X and has been working for the department for twenty years. Marcia is in her late fifties.

Patricia is a white retired elementary teacher and part-time adjunct faculty member (non-terminal degree). Patricia is in her early sixties.

The Department

A leader's character and behavior have a direct effect on the climate of an organization. There are many different conceptions of ethical leadership, both inside and outside of education. Strodi (1992) defines leadership as "the influence a person asserts upon the behavior of others . . . the quality of a person to motivate people to change individual behavior to cooperative group behavior and to give direction and purpose to the lives of other people" (p. 3). Some find leadership difficult to define, let alone "ethical leadership," but they "know it when they see it."

As Wahlstrom and Seashore Louis (2008) state, "teacher, custodian, education assistant, specialist, office support staff—they all seem to know good (and bad) leadership when they experience it. Furthermore, most people can identify particular behaviors of school leaders that they remember as being effective" (p. 459). Not all "bad" leaders are unethical, but all unethical leaders are "bad" leaders.

However, popular texts on leadership used in university schools of education and educational leadership often do not make mention of women's leadership, how gender plays a large part in people's conceptions of leaders, how authentic leaders appear to their followers (which is often impacted by gender and other uncontrollable characteristics such as race, class, and sexuality), or the unique challenges women and individuals possessing minority or multiple minority statuses face as leaders in education.

That being said, one's standpoint is relevant to this conversation, whether it be the leader's standpoint or the standpoint of others in the organization; our standpoint informs our points of view and often either enables or inhibits our goal attainment.

Relational-cultural theory accords quite nicely with the transformational leadership model, a leadership model considered to be ideal for educational settings, and provides for relational leadership and value for the communal, for mentoring, and for establishing a sense of connection between people. Transformational leadership is often considered to be the most effective style of leadership because it is premised on the building of empowerment in a mutual and collaborative context (Eagly & Carli, 2007; Eagly, Johannesen-Schmidt, & van Engen, 2003).

As program director of the master's program, Franklin is the lone decider of the professors chosen to work in the program. His leadership style is decidedly non-transformational and non-collaborative. He selected Susan and Sara, both untenured and working in the undergraduate program at University X, to work in the master's program. He also hired a third young woman to work in the master's program, Dominique. A year after Dominique was hired, Franklin hired another woman, Judith, to work in both the graduate and the undergraduate programs.

Franklin's leadership style relies heavily on allocating duties and many of the responsibilities of program director to his faculty. Susan and Sara handle marketing, accreditation, and admissions. When Dominique was hired, the three women worked on licensure for the master's program as well as program accreditation. To wit, Franklin has been known to state that he "likes to hire women because they work harder."

Franklin has also been known to make comments about women's appearance, clothing, and make-up. He tells female students not to wear their engagement rings/wedding rings when interviewing for jobs. He often makes sexist statements and then states, to whom he was speaking, "Sorry." Or before making one, "I know this isn't politically correct, but . . ."

Franklin makes disparaging comments about female colleagues as well as women all over campus in terms of clothing, make-up, and hair. He says nothing about the men at the university who dress informally or sloppily. Franklin refers to the three blonde women working with him in the graduate program as his "Charlie's Angels," with himself taking on the role of Charlie; Dominique is the "odd woman out" of this metaphor.

In the department, there is a growing concern about disparities in the experiences of male and female employees with a pattern of inequitable division of labor (with women doing the lion's share of the work), as well as a hostile work environment for women who hear Franklin's negative and disparaging comments. Franklin's leadership style was of particular concern to Judith when it came to Dominique.

During a department meeting at the beginning of spring semester, Franklin indicated that the dean requires faculty to be on campus five days per week. Dominique asked a question about this, because she had heard conflicting messages about this institutional norm. Franklin yelled at Dominique in this meeting, telling her not to question him.

He also stated that the dean just told him that all faculty are required to be on campus five days per week, and that Dominique should go over and ask her if she did not believe him. Dominique said nothing in response. Although faculty members in the department get visibly upset when Franklin yells at colleagues, the normal response is for everyone to put their heads down and not look directly at Franklin or the person to whom he is addressing.

The day after this meeting, three female faculty members (two junior and one senior) and one staff member came to Dominique separately to check on her and to offer their support. They all stated that Franklin's actions were unfair, unwarranted, and inappropriate.

Dominique later found out from the dean herself that Franklin's claims were untrue. When the female senior faculty member came to show her support to Dominique, she asserted that Franklin was a "male chauvinist" and that she had problems with him in the past. Dominique did not ask her colleague to reveal any details about her prior experiences with Franklin. However, she did appreciate the support.

Dominique emailed Franklin a few days later and requested a meeting to discuss his behavior toward her at the department meeting. He did not respond. A day after this, she went to his office to inquire whether he had received the email. He looked surprised. He stated, "What email? I get a lot of emails. What was it about?"

She stated, "I want to talk about what happened at the meeting earlier in the week." Dominique proceeded to tell him that she did not appreciate being yelled at, particularly in front of colleagues.

He stated that he was not talking to her when speaking of the dean's directive to be on campus five days per week, and that she was inappropriate because she had interrupted him when he was speaking to someone else. Dominique indicated that this was untrue.

At this point, Franklin's face began to redden. His tone grew immediately angry and aggressive, and he began to critique Dominique's performance and demeanor in general, "When someone interrupts me, they are likely to be yelled at. What you did was out of bounds. I was not even speaking to you."

Dominique then stated, "Well, I am not the only one who feels that you spoke to me inappropriately."

He then stated, "We can go tit for tat, Dominique."

She asked, "What do you mean?"

Franklin spoke, "Well, I think I had better not say."

She replied, "You opened the door; walk through it."

At a faculty meeting a few days earlier, the full faculty was debating what it would mean for faculty to collaborate. Having great experience with team teaching and collaborating across disciplines, Dominique raised her hand to speak.

The faculty had desired to define the term collaboration in general and what this would mean for them. Dominique did so. Franklin then stated, "One of your senior colleagues in this department came to me and expressed concern about you speaking up. And I am not making this up, Dominique."

She stated, "Well, I am sure they just have my best interest in mind—and they are just looking out for me."

He stated, "I just want to make sure you will be able to keep your job."

She stated, "I consider that a threat."

He stated, "If you do not want me to mentor you, then fine."

She said, "I need to be viewed as a peer, as a colleague. I think that I am doing everything I need to be doing, and if I feel that I should speak up, I will."

Dominique later spoke to the senior faculty in the department about what was said during her meeting with Franklin and learned that none of her senior colleagues were in attendance at the faculty meeting when she spoke. All had either left early or were not in attendance.

A few hours later, Franklin came to her office, apologized, and shook her hand. He said that he had been thinking about their meeting for hours and felt terrible. He ended with, "Are we okay?" Dominique was shocked by this, but she considered it a victory. She deemed this apology as Franklin's realization that he had stepped over the line. She accepted his apology, shook his hand, and hoped all would be well.

Upon reflection, Dominique thought she should create a paper trail, not only of Franklin's threat, but also of the inequitable division of labor in the department based on gender. Although she was fearful as a new faculty member, she made an appointment to speak with the dean.

The dean was welcoming to her concerns. Dominique shared the above incidents, as well as her concerns about Franklin evaluating her. She questioned whether Franklin would be fair with her. Dominique communicated to the dean her perceptions of a hostile work environment. The dean communicated that she would keep an eye on the situation and placed documentation of this meeting in Dominique's file in case any future incidents transpired.

The Review

In February, Franklin called Dominique into his office indicating that he wanted to prep with her before her second-year review with the dean, which was to occur the Monday after classes resumed following spring break. During this meeting, Franklin said *nothing* constructive to her (although she was renewed without conditions by the faculty personnel committee).

Franklin stated, "I think you are really effective with the undergraduate students, but you are not effective with graduate students." Upon hearing this, Dominique expressed shock. Franklin continued, "A graduate student, and I am not going to say who, wrote a letter to me, speaking for the entire cohort, complaining about your performance as a professor, and I am not making this up."

Again, Dominique expressed shock. She asked, "When did this occur?"

Franklin stated, "A while back."

Dominique asked, "Why was I not informed of this? Who wrote this letter and can I see it?"

Franklin refused to either produce the letter, reveal who the writer was, or share the specific complaints about her. Additionally, Franklin had never previously indicated to her anything about student complaints.

A week later, after returning from spring break, Dominique attended her second-year review meeting with the dean and Franklin. Dominique was terrified that Franklin would share this letter with the dean, of which she questioned the veracity, but Franklin said nothing negative. The meeting went well. However, Dominique learned that Franklin placed job postings into her mailbox and made comments to the administrative staff, for example, "Here's hoping that Dominique will leave."

Departmental Norms

On a departmental workday in April, called by Susan, Dominique was paired with David, a male co-worker, to assess student teachers' edTPA portfolios. Student teachers at University X are required to upload videos of their teaching, as well as data, student work, and self-assessments of their experiences with student teaching.

Faculty at University X cancelled classes for two days so that they could assess all of the electronic portfolios of their student teachers. Prior to these meetings, Patricia warned Dominique that David "does very little" and that she needed to be "strong" with him. To be proactive, Dominique emailed David a few weeks before they were scheduled to conduct these assessments.

Dominique informed David that she would be out of town during the first day of these assessments at a conference and asked how he wanted to divide the workload. He never responded. Instead, he called Dominique after the first workday to inform her that he does not check his university email and requested that she come in early on the second workday so that they could get the scoring accomplished.

Upon arriving on the second day, Dominique learned that David had done nothing the day before, because she was not there. He stated that he did not have a computer in order to complete the work (although there was a computer lab across the hall from the meeting room). He also did not bring a computer on the second day. Although Franklin was a part of an assessment team, he neither came to these meetings nor did he participate in the scoring. Susan organized these meetings and was present at them, but she did not assign herself to an assessment team.

Dominique then escorted David to the computer lab across the hall and asked him to log in so that they could equitably divide their tasks. He indicated that he did not know how. David was not a new employee and had participated in similar scoring teams in previous years, although not with Dominique. Dominique subsequently logged in to the computer using her own username and password and then asked David to log into the assessment site. David pleaded ignorance. Dominique stated, "I will be right back."

Dominique stepped out of the meeting to find two of her female colleagues, Susan and Marcia, standing in the hallway. She whispered emphatically to them, "This situation is absolutely unacceptable. I cannot take this inequity. This is bullshit. I am not going to do this man's work for him. This goes on too much, and no one says anything because it's *easier*. I just can't do it anymore."

Dominique then asked Susan, since she was not part of an assessment team, to assist David with technology. She asked that Susan assist David with the assessment website. She then divided the work equitably, so that each had two students to assess. Dominique assessed two and informed David of the other two students he should assess. Dominique completed her work.

In May, Judith pulled Dominique into an empty office on campus and shut the door. She shared with Dominique that Franklin had confessed to her that he hoped Dominique would either be hired elsewhere or would simply quit. Dominique looked at Judith, both shock and concern apparent on her face.

Judith explained, "Franklin likes me. I laugh at his jokes. He always confesses his sins to me, so to speak. But what he is doing is wrong, and I just had to tell you. Do you remember that assessment day when you were paired with David?" Dominique nodded.

"Well," Judith continued, "Franklin filed a complaint against you. He told human resources that you yelled and swore at David. He indicated that we cannot have aggressive faculty who yell and swear in front of community members out in the open. He then had David, Marcia, and Patricia go over to human resources and sign statements to this effect. He made the appointments for them to do so. He admitted all of this to me. I just wanted to give you a head's up. You are going to be called into HR next week. I think he wants you to explode. I thought you should know so that you will be prepared."

The Dilemma

Dominique feels that any time she disagrees or asks a question, Franklin responds with anger and retaliatory behavior. She considers this to be a hostile working environment on many fronts. Dominique is the lone untenured faculty member of color in the department.

As the "only," working in a predominantly white institution, she is terrified of broaching issues of race in an environment that may be hostile. She is also concerned about being painted as the stereotype of the "Angry Black Woman." Additionally, Franklin has never observed Dominique's teaching in her two years at the university.

TEACHING NOTES

This case is based on Educational Leadership Constituent Council Standard 5.0:

> An educational leader promotes the success of every student by acting with integrity, fairness, and in an ethical manner to ensure every student's academic and social success by modeling organizational principles of self-awareness, reflective practice, transparency, and ethical behavior; safeguarding the values of democracy, equity, and diversity; evaluating the potential moral and legal consequences of decision making; and promoting social justice to ensure individual student needs inform all aspects of schooling. (Educational Leadership Constituent Council, 2011, p. 18)

This standard was informed by research that emphasized the critical importance in creating, nurturing, and sustaining a culture and climate that upholds the values and beliefs of the organization, adheres to the laws and regulations of the state, and rests on the moral principles of justice and fairness.

Ethics originate from the Greek word *ethos*, meaning character, conduct, and/or customs (Rowe & Guerrero, 2012). Ethics reflect the morals and values of a society and help individuals determine what is right and wrong in any given situation. With respect to leadership, ethics is about who leaders are—an ethical leader is one who is committed to the pursuit of truth, and is fair and just in their decision making, actions, attitudes, and interactions with others (Educational Leadership Constituent Council, 2011; Rawls, 1971).

Ethics is central to leadership because of the inherent relationship between leaders and followers (Rowe & Guerrero, 2012). Leaders can influence the lives of followers either negatively or positively, and the direction of that effect depends on the leaders' character and behavior (Yukl, 2012). With leadership comes a great obligation to recognize each person as an individual, with their own distinctive identity, and to treat each person with dignity and respect.

Finally, leaders are instrumental in developing and establishing organizational values. Their own personal values determine the type of ethical climate that will develop in their organizations. The paramount responsibility of an educational leader is to develop a school culture characterized by empathy, trust, and support that will serve faculty when faced with difficult situations (Heifetz, 1994; Northouse, 2013; Yukl, 2012).

Because of the diverse makeup of schools, educational leaders must possess sufficient knowledge of the laws and policies enacted by local, state, and federal authorities that guarantee equal opportunities to faculty and students, and organizational policies related to the rights with respect to groups of individuals who share a particular race, language, sex, poverty, or disability (Lopez, 2003).

This knowledge will influence and shape a leader's decision making and leadership styles. Effective leaders are advocates for students, families, and faculty who uphold the democratic values of equity and equality. When challenges arise, leaders must help followers reach higher ethical standards (Burns, 1978).

Reflective practice promotes self-awareness, ethical behavior, and professional growth over time (Sparks, 2005). When engaging in reflective practice, leaders are able to gain a greater perception of their personal beliefs, values, motivations, and actions in relation to the desired goals or administrative decisions that define their performance.

Reflection requires individuals to accept responsibility for their actions and to adapt leadership strategies and practices, and thereby contribute to a more effective environment for learning.

QUESTIONS FOR DISCUSSION

The following questions were written to initiate classroom discussion and help current and future leadership practitioners raise their awareness of their own beliefs, values, and ethical foundations. The ethical challenges and moral responsibilities that come with the power of leadership are examined.

1. Is hair color relevant? Franklin has hired three youngish blond women to work in the master's program. The only woman not fitting this "type" is Dominique, and she was subject to unfair treatment. Does this treatment pertain to race or her questioning of the status quo, or both? What recourse does Dominique have? Does this case imply unfairness on the part of Franklin to other members of the department?

2. Dominique is confident that there are gender inequities in her department. Should she pursue the issue of racial inequity as well as gender inequity? What potential dangers could she place herself in if she pursues racial discrimination? What protections does she have?

3. Possessing an ethical character involves possessing the values that guide our choices and include trustworthiness, respect, responsibility, fairness, caring, and citizenship. Virtues and vices are typically understood as dispositions that lead us to act or behave in certain ways. How would the faculty describe Franklin's character and behavior?

4. Social justice involves fairness and equity, and represents a perspective in regard to how "fundamental rights and duties are assigned and on the economic opportunities and social conditions" (Rawls, 1971, p. 7). As a full tenured professor, does Franklin have the right to ask untenured and part-time faculty and staff to do the work that he is unwilling to do? Should Dominique be expected to take on additional work because she is untenured?

5. How would you define Franklin's leadership style?

6. A leader's knowledge of local, state, and national policy knowledge enables leaders to implement and evaluate policies, procedures, and practices within their organizations in compliance with the law (Waters & Marzano, 2006). How does Title IX apply to this case?[1] Is this a case of sex discrimination? Why or why not? Does Dominique have any recourse as an untenured faculty member? What are the consequences of Franklin's behavior: for the group, for Franklin, for the university, for Dominique? Should Dominique take legal action against Franklin?

7. The dean holds a position of authority with administrative responsibilities for the College of Education. A dean oversees all personnel matters involving academic and non-academic employees. What is the dean's role in this case? Should the dean have followed up with Dominique after the initial meeting where Dominique made allegations against Franklin? What are her professional and ethical responsibilities? Did she follow these?

8. Teleological theory is related to the consequences of a leader's actions, behavior, and/or conduct. There are three approaches to assessing outcomes. First, *ethical egoism* describes actions that are designed to obtain the greatest good for the leader. Second, *utilitarianism* refers to the actions that are designed to obtain the greatest good for the largest number of people. Third, *altruism* describes actions that are designed to demonstrate concern for others' interests, even if these interests are contrary to the leader's self-interests.

    Create a table. In the first column, identify Franklin's actions, behaviors, and/or conduct throughout the case. In the second column, determine the consequences or outcomes for each action, behavior, and conduct listed in the first column. In the third column, label each consequence as ethical egoistic, utilitarian, or altruistic.

9. Assess this case using a model of ethical leadership.

ADDITIONAL ACTIVITIES

This case was developed for a course on organizational leadership with a focus on ethical and legal implications. In this case, Franklin is the chair of the department and the program director for the master's program in educational leadership. Dominique has recently joined the department as an untenured member of the faculty.

One of the salient questions is whether Dominique specifically and other department faculty and staff in general have been subject to inequitable treatment under Franklin's leadership. Unethical leaders expect those with less power to do the work that they are unwilling to do themselves (e.g., work that they view to be "beneath them"). Ethical leaders lead by example and demonstrate their expectations of others through clear guidance.

As a follow-up to classroom discussion, students can be asked to write a case analysis and follow up with small group discussion to compare their analyses. To guide, students are recommended to follow some generic steps: 1) Identify the key actors and the role they play in this case study, 2) Identify the plot line—what happened? 3) What are the issues of this case? 4) Identify the causes and effects of each action. What actions (if any) served to escalate the situation? What actions (if any) served to remedy the situation? 5) What theory can you draw upon to explain what happened in this case?

Furthermore, making good ethical decisions requires a trained sensitivity to ethical issues. Having a method for ethical decision making is helpful for practitioners. Have students work in small groups to develop a framework for ethical decision making that will serve as a useful tool for exploring ethical dilemmas and identifying courses of action. Additional resources that may provide context for the case and class discussion include:

Monroe, S. (2007). *Dear colleague letter.* Washington, DC: U.S. Department of Education Office for Civil Rights. http://www2.ed.gov/about/offices/list/ocr/letters/colleague-20070622.pdf.
Marcus, K. (2004). *Title IX grievance procedures, postsecondary education.* Washington, DC: U.S. Department of Education Office for Civil Rights. http://www2.ed.gov/about/offices/list/ocr/responsibilities_ix_ps.html.

NOTE

1. See the following reference for assistance with the civil rights protections that may pertain to this case: U.S. Department of Education Office for Civil Rights. (2010, October 26). *Letter to colleagues.* http://www2.ed.gov/about /offices/list/ocr/letters/colleague-201010.pdf.

REFERENCES

Burns, J. M. (1978). *Leadership.* New York, NY: Harper & Row.

Darling-Hammond, L. (1988). Policy and professionalism. In A. Lieberman (Ed.), *Building a professional culture in* schools (pp. 55–77). New York, NY: Teachers College Press.

Eagly, A., & Carli, L. L. (2007). *Through the labyrinth: The truth about how women become leaders.* Boston, MA: Harvard Business School Press.

Eagly, A. H., and Johannessen-Schmidt, M. C., & van Engen, M. L. (2003). Transformational, transactional, and laissez-faire leadership styles: A meta-analysis comparing women and men. *Psychological Bulletin,* 129(4), 569–591.

Educational Leadership Constituent Council. (2011). Educational Leadership Program Standards. *National Policy Board for Educational Administration.* http://www.ncate.org/LinkClick.aspx?fileticket=zRZI73R0nOQ%3D&tabid=676.

Heifetz, R. A. (1994). *Leadership without easy answers.* Cambridge, MA: Harvard University Press.

Klein, S. (Ed.). (2007). *Handbook for achieving gender equity through education* (2nd ed.). Hillsdale, NJ: Erlbaum Publishers.

Lopez, G. (2003). The (racially neutral) politics of education: A critical race theory perspective. *Educational Administration Quarterly,* 39(1), 68–94.

Martin, J., Kearl, H., & Murphy, W. J. (2013). Bullying and harassment in schools: Analysis of legislation and policy. In M. A. Paludi (Ed.), *Women and management: Global issues and promising solutions. Volume 2: Signs of solutions* (pp. 29–51). Santa Barbara, CA: Praeger.

Northouse, P. G. (2013). *Leadership: Theory and practice* (6th ed.) Thousand Oaks, CA: Sage.

Pittard, M., & Butler, D. (2008). Liberally educated teachers and the culture of niceness: Findings from a qualitative study in liberal arts and secondary teaching. In M. Pittard, D. Butler, & J, McDowell (Eds.), *Liberal arts education and teacher education: A lasting relationship* (pp. 69–90). http://www.ailacte.org/images/uploads/general/monograph_opt.pdf.

Rawls, J. (1971). *A theory of justice.* Cambridge, MA: Belknap Press of Harvard University Press.

Rowe, G. W., & Guerrero, L. (2012). *Cases in leadership (Ivey Casebook Serires).* (3rd ed.). Sage Publications, Inc. 1-528.

Sparks, D. (2005). *Leading for results: Transforming teaching, learning and relationships in schools.* Thousand Oaks, CA: Corwin Press.

Strodi, P. (1992, March). *A model of teacher leadership.* Paper presented at the Eastern Educational Research Association Annual Meeting, Hilton Head, SC.

U.S. Census Bureau. (2010). American FactFinder. http://factfinder2.census.gov/faces/nav/jsf/pages/index.xhtml.

U.S. Department of Education Office of Civil Rights. (2010, October 26). Dear colleague letter: Harassment and bullying. http://www2.ed.gov/about/offices/list/ocr/letters/colleague-201010.pdf.

Wahlstrom, K. L., & Seashore Louis, K. (2008). How teachers experience principal leadership: The roles of professional community, trust, efficacy, and shared responsibility. *Educational Administration Quarterly,* 44(4), 458–95.

Yukl, G. (2012). *Leadership in organizations* (8th ed.). Upper Saddle River, NJ: Pearson/Prentice Hall.

Chapter Ten

The Effects of Open Enrollment on Easton High School

INTRODUCTION

School choice and the use of vouchers for education have fueled the expansion of virtual online charter schools. This redirection of tax dollars contributes to the idea that virtual school success is comparable or even superior to the performance of traditional public schools, and to the misperception that virtual charter schools and traditional public schools are subject to the same governmental oversight. The schools most adversely affected by this practice are the schools with the highest need, those serving children living in poverty and underserved minority student populations: urban public schools.

School choice is a critical component of educational reform efforts across the country that attempt to provide students in failing schools the opportunity to obtain a high-quality education. Each state develops its own formula to redistribute state tax revenue to local schools. These formulae are designed to correct funding imbalances that might otherwise occur if public schools had to solely rely on local taxes for funding.

With educational reform founding a system where parents are permitted to select the school their child attends, public money is diverted away from public schools and given to community schools. Darling-Hammond (2013) argues that continued de facto segregation contributes to the disproportionate funding of public schools, creating a continued disadvantage to urban schools in particular, which comprise higher concentrations of students of color and students living in poverty.

High-poverty schools are those where at least 75 percent of the student population receives free and reduced price lunch; a disproportionate number of high-poverty schools are located in urban centers and consist of higher percentages of Latina/o and Black students (Berends, 2014).

Competition between the public and private sectors further exacerbates inequities in funding that most negatively impact urban schools. Touted as vehicles to improve schools, the large expansion of virtual online charter schools has resulted from the privatization of public funds for education through the use of tax credits and vouchers (Miron, Horvitz, & Gulosino, 2013). Online schools receive funding based on enrollment numbers using a base per pupil amount that follows each student, not on the cost of education (Barbour, 2012).

This reallocation of funding away from public schools has an adverse effect, leaving many public schools, particularly urban public schools, under-funded (Berends, 2014; Dixon, Royal, & Henry, 2014). This case examines the inequitable funding impacting public schools within the context of the redistribution of public monies from public to online community schools, and also looks into the lack of oversight in charter schools today.

THE CASE

Easton High School is considered a high-needs school as indicated by student achievement data and student demographics. Easton High School has remained at the level of Academic Emergency for the last four years, with an enrollment of 1,246 students and approximately 29 percent of the population receiving special education services.

For the 2013-2014 School Year Report Card, no state indicators were met and 70.7 points out of 120 were earned on the Performance Index. This building serves 100 percent economically disadvantaged students, of which 98 percent are African American, non-Hispanic, and 1.6 percent are white, non-Hispanic.

The attendance rate has shown improvement and increased from 87.8 percent in 2010 to 89.3 percent in 2013. However, the graduation rate declined from 71.9 percent in 2008-2009 to 53.4 percent in 2011-2012, but increased to 61.4 percent in 2013-2014. In 2014, 45.2 percent of the tenth-grade students passed the Ohio Graduation Test, while the state requirement is 75 percent. A decline in student performance for this urban high school is clearly indicated.

Over the past four years, Easton has had nearly three hundred students open enroll into nearby charter schools and virtual online charter schools. Like district public schools, these schools are funded according to enrollment (also called average daily attendance), and receive funding from the district and the state based on the number of students attending. Last year, more than

$2,250,000 in school funding was transferred from Easton High School to virtual charter schools.

The redistribution of resources as a result of school choice has left Easton High School a struggling district with fewer resources, making it even more difficult to meet the diverse needs of their learners. This has led to larger class sizes, personnel cuts, declining morale, and heightened disparity. The loss of these funds has placed a burden on the principal to tighten the budget. He has also had to lay off some teachers at the start of the school year because of declining enrollment at the eleventh hour.

Student Characteristics

The percentage of African American students served by charter schools and virtual charter schools is lower than the state average: 8.8 percent of the virtual school enrollment is African American, while 15.9 percent of all public school students are African American.

There are more girls (53 percent) than boys (47 percent) enrolled in charter schools. Students who qualify for free or reduced-price lunch in charter schools is 7.75 percentage points lower than the average for all public schools: 39.65 percent compared with 47.4 percent. In general, charter schools serve a lower percentage of economically disadvantaged students than conventional public schools. Overall, the proportion of students with disabilities in virtual schools is a little lower than the state average or 12.18 percent compared with 14.8 percent.

The Problem

Principal Joseph Monroe knew from previous years the challenges open enrollment placed on his school, but this year he was experiencing a new phenomenon. This year, there was an incursion of students returning to Easton Middle School. The first day of school was only five days away.

Teachers had already been hired and placed, students were assigned to classes, and schedules mailed, but in the last week forty-seven students reenrolled. Almost all of the students were returning from online virtual charter schools.

Principal Monroe would have to answer many questions. What are the class enrollments presently, and how do they comply with the master contract? It is possible that one or more additional teachers will be needed to accommodate the increased enrollment? The addition of intervention specialists, even on a part-time basis, may be required to meet student need. These are monetary considerations, which will require immediate action given the time of year.

The return of students from charter schools will increase revenue from the state; however, it may not be enough to cover the total cost to the district. Another administrative concern would be the availability of quality teachers at this time.

To advertise for staff, interview, and research candidate credentials on such short notice places great pressure on administrators. Resolving this situation will take considerable administrative time and planning so as to provide educationally sound placements and programming, including defensible decisions for parents.

The Local Paper

Because so much public funding is being redirected from Easton into virtual charter schools, the editor of the local newspaper, *The Vindicator*, felt it was important that parents had the information they needed to compare the performance of the public school to the online charter schools.

Seasoned reporter Randy Hoover volunteered to conduct an investigation. Randy felt it was his job to tell the *real* story behind these "failing" schools. Randy came from a family of teachers, and he had seen firsthand how hard they worked throughout his life. He was dismayed at the assault on teachers and public schools. He saw how higher expectations and decreases in benefits, as well as lack of classroom resources, impacted his loved ones and made their jobs more difficult.

Randy believed that there were political, policy, and societal issues and problems that impacted teacher's abilities to do their jobs well, and that blaming "bad" teachers, teacher unions, and teacher tenure within the popular media was only passing the buck, and he resented this. Randy sought to tell the true story of teachers and what they faced within their classrooms as well as to investigate the problems that plagued schools deemed as failing, beyond the micro level of individual responsibility. He embraced the challenge of telling the story at the meso and macro levels.

The report by Randy Hoover published in *The Vindicator* informed readers that students enrolled in online charter schools demonstrated significantly lower achievement gains than students in Easton High School. Hoover argued that school choice options have not been shown to increase student achievement and there is extensive difficulty associated with the ability of researchers to evaluate achievement outcomes for charter schools in general (Ledwith, 2010).

Out of twenty-three online charter schools in the state, only three (13 percent) were rated effective or higher on the state report card compared with 75 percent of brick-and-mortar schools. Approximately 97 percent of traditional school districts are rated higher and had better graduation rates than the seven statewide virtual charter schools. Given the rapid growth of virtual schools and their relatively poor performance, Hoover argued, these findings have great implications for urban education specifically and for education policy in general.

Returning Student Performance

Several issues related to the return of students from charters to Easton were of concern to Principal Monroe. Their last minute return created issues with scheduling and program implementation. Principal Monroe was tasked to find out how far behind the incoming students were. How many of them would require "special programming"?

Administratively, how would he determine where to place each returning student? What criteria would be used? There were just enough students to create the need for several new faculty hires, but the pool of prospective hires would already be picked over by this late date.

Furthermore, the academic records from the students returning from on-line schools indicated that students did not have the support needed to work in an online learning environment. Students appeared to have struggled with the online courses and their grades were low at mostly Cs and Ds. The high attrition rate was a significant indicator of student distress. Teachers at Easton High School had their work cut out for them in the coming school year, remediating the students from the poor academic experiences they had in the previous year.

After reading Gerald Hoover's article in *The Vindicator*, Principal Monroe, feeling slightly vindicated, decided to contact Mr. Hoover to offer an interview. Principal Monroe desired to communicate the implications of the real failing schools, virtual online charters in Ohio, that were not gaining any press. Gerald Hoover readily agreed and met Principal Monroe at his school to conduct the interview.

As the two sat down to speak, Principal Monroe was already impassioned. "Mr. Hoover, I very much appreciated your article. Schools, in particular schools like ours—struggling urban schools—do not often enjoy good press. Thank you for writing an honest article." Mr. Hoover nodded modestly as Principal Monroe continued, "These virtual charters, and charter schools in general for that matter, were touted as vehicles to improve the education of our most challenged students, but that was an elaborate ruse.

After all, it was Albert Shanker, president of the United Federation of Teachers from 1964 to 1985, who originally conceived of this idea. But, his idea involved charters as vehicles to assist the public schools, not compete with them. His vision was that charter schools would serve as lab schools, schools that would experiment with cutting edge pedagogies and then share their ideas with the public schools. Not many people know this.

The real story is this: online schools receive funding based on enrollment numbers using a base per pupil amount that follows each student, not on the cost of education. We both know brick-and-mortar schools cost more. But this reallocation of funding away from public schools has an adverse effect, leaving many public schools, particularly urban public schools, underfunded. They are failing more than we, but they do not have the oversight that we have. It is not apples to apples."

Mr. Hoover nodded again. "I am with you on all of this, and I agree 100 percent. But, I am a reporter. I know what most folks will respond to. I want to make your case for you, but we need a face for this story. If we do not have a story of a student, or a group of students who have been directly impacted by this, then there is no story. I mean, I want to hear you speak, but the general public? Not so much."

"Let me get this straight," Principal Monroe began, "The story needs to be about kids being disadvantaged and not about the politicians who have built their careers and the lobbyists who have lined their pockets by taking public funds and moving them to private entities? Do I have that right?"

"Pretty much," Mr. Hoover replied sheepishly, without returning Principal Monroe's gaze.

"Well, then, respectfully, I think this interview is over. You are the reporter. Find your story. You know that ethically I cannot divulge any information about specific students or their experiences. If you ever want my take on this, my door is open, but I cannot help you with the human interest angle you are looking for. However, I do hope that you find it. On your own. And I hope that you will be able to tell this important story."

Mr. Hoover left the interview feeling a bit dressed down, but challenged. Never one to back down from a challenge, he wrote an editorial in the next week's paper asking for stories about student experiences with local charter schools. His email inbox became inundated with responses. After corresponding with several parents, he thought he found the one story that would enable him to break the truth of charters.

Mr. Hoover met with Ms. Simmons, a former charter school parent, the following week and she reiterated her son's story, which she had previously shared via email. Ms. Simmons's son Sam is twelve years old and just finished the sixth grade. At what the family perceived as being the beginning of Sam's seventh grade year, Ms. Simmons was informed in late July that Sam would be retained, without any advance warning. Ms. Simmons had attempted to communicate with the appropriate school official, Director of Exceptional Education and Student Advocate Ms. Aquino.

Ms. Aquino had previously sent a letter to Ms. Simmons indicating that Sam experienced frustration with the curriculum, engaged in obsessive talking, displayed delayed responses, did not listen, and possessed a lack of focus.

Ms. Simmons indicated to Mr. Hoover that she had consulted the student handbook and learned that student services were available for children who experience learning challenges. However, no interventions were ever made for her son. Ms. Simmons made several attempts to contact Ms. Aquino, both via phone and email. She did not receive a response until one month later, in August, one week before school was to begin. She was informed that nothing could be done and that Sam was scheduled to repeat the sixth grade.

Sam returned to the school, repeating sixth grade, without any successful resolution of the issues at hand. In September, Ms. Simmons accompanied her son to the school and demanded answers and resolution. Ms. Aquino met with her and assured her that the sixth-grade learning specialist was working on a learning plan for Sam. Ten days later, Ms. Simmons received an email from Ms. Aquino indicating that the learning specialist was still working on the learning plan and that the school would be in touch soon.

Ms. Simmons immediately requested that her son be tested for special education services. Meanwhile, Sam's grades continued to decline. The educational plan that the family received included enrolling Sam in a required Saturday School Academy, which did not address any of his basic skill issues.

Ms. Simmons was later informed that Sam would have to complete three sets of informational packets per subject that ranged from two to three hundred pages each, with no assistance from the school. In addition, when all of the packets were completed, Sam was required to take a series of two exams per subject and pass them all in order to be promoted.

Ms. Simmons questioned whether staff would be available to assist Sam with the completion of these packets during Saturday school. Although the Student Handbook clearly indicated that mechanisms were available to assist students in the successful completion of the school's rigorous curriculum, Ms. Simmons's requests were either ignored or denied.

Mr. Hoover wondered if this was a common experience with children experiencing learning challenges in charter schools. "What was the resolution of this situation?"

"They pretended that many of these conversations had never happened. They essentially did nothing to assist my son. Ultimately, everyone within the Office of Exceptional Education and Student Advocates allowed this African American child to fail. And we are still in litigation on this. I fear for the future of my child. I am confident that I now have him in a school that actually cares about his academic success, but I am terrified about the potential irreparable damage that his three years in this charter may have caused."

Mr. Hoover left the interview feeling that he had the story he needed to tell. He thought about what he would write for what he deemed a necessary and relevant human interest story. In order to communicate the negative aspects of charters and their devastating impact not only on public schools (and specifically on urban public schools), but also on the children who attend them, he felt a profound sadness, but also anger at the untold numbers of children being ill served by educational policy and politics.

TEACHING NOTES

Competition between the public and private sectors further exacerbates inequities in funding that most negatively impact urban schools. Critics assert that school choice policies benefit the most advantaged families (Lavery, 2012), leaving regular public schools with diminished resources to meet the needs of students with the greatest needs for support and intervention (Carr, 2011; Hubard, 2014; Moe, 2008). Research has found a correlation between low student performance and socio-economic status: as a school's percentage of low-income students increases, the ability to raise funds decreases (Howe, Eisenhart, & Betebenner, 2001).

The amount districts receive for open enrolled students is only slightly higher than the marginal cost of educating an additional student (Reback, 2008). Ultimately, school choice may be potentially damaging to both districts and individual students (Jimerson, 2002). Skimming can occur in which high-performing students are pulled away from low-achieving districts, resulting in the isolation of underperforming students in underperforming schools without the funds necessary to meet such needs (Howe, Eisenhart, & Betebenner, 2001).

School choice also leads to increases in student mobility and transiency which has been shown to have a negative impact on student achievement (Lavery & Carlson, 2012). High mobility levels make it impossible for districts to anticipate budgets from year to year, limiting their ability to innovate and improve.

Declines in funding because of school choice initiatives have caused many public districts to become open enrollment providers (Fowler, 1996). Other districts suffering enrollment declines have been forced to defer maintenance; cut programs and teachers in areas such as art, music, and physical education; eliminate programs in elementary school such as foreign language and science; decrease positions of special education assistants; cut field trips; reduce guidance counselor positions; and eliminate advanced courses in math and science courses in high schools (Jimerson, 2002).

As Malugade (2014) argues, "Any attempt to rationalize the less than optimal education received by students left behind in the losing districts fails to take into consideration the fundamental state constitutional guarantee of '[a]n equal opportunity for a sound basic education'" (p. 850).

Touted as vehicles to improve schools, the large expansion of virtual online charter schools has resulted from the privatization of public funds for education through the use of tax credits and vouchers (Miron, Horvitz, & Gulosino, 2013). Online schools receive funding based on enrollment numbers using a base per pupil amount that follows each student, not on the cost of education (Barbour, 2012). This reallocation of funding away from public schools has an adverse effect, leaving many public schools, particularly urban public schools, underfunded (Berends, 2014; Dixon, Royal, & Henry, 2014).

QUESTIONS FOR DISCUSSION

1. Research the historical and political factors that have led to school choice and open enrollment. What systemic effects are the results of these initiatives? What participation effects are the results of these initiatives?
2. Based on the data presented in the case, are white students disproportionately leaving public schools to attend virtual schools? How does school choice affect student segregation (by race, ethnicity, and income)?
3. What should the findings of the online charter school performance investigation have on public policy?
4. Critics of school choice suggest there is perhaps a false assumption that parents will select schools based on academic quality (Jacobs, 2011). Many parents are likely to make choices based on proximity regardless of demographic composition (Jacobs, 2011).

    Other research has shown that parent choices are made based on factors such as race, class, more segregated opportunities (Moe, 2008), curricular focus, extracurricular activities, safety, and convenience (Ni, 2012). Based on this research, how can public schools help parents make more informed decisions when it comes to school choice?
5. What can Principal Monroe do to inform parents of these findings before they remove their students from Easton High School?
6. How would Ms. Simmons's experience have been different if her son had attended a traditional public school?

REFERENCES

Barbour, M. (2012). Virtual schools are more cost-effective compared to traditional brick-and-mortar schools? In K. P. Brady (Ed.), *Technology in schools* (pp. 84–90). Los Angeles, CA: Sage.

Berends, M. (2014). The evolving landscape of school choice in the United States. In H. R. Milner IV & K. Lomotey (Eds.), *Handbook of urban education* (pp. 451–73). New York, NY: Routledge.

Carr, M. (2011). The impact of Ohio's edchoice on traditional public school performance. *CATO Journal, 31*(2), 257–84.

Darling-Hammond. L. (2013). Diversity, equity, and education in a globalized world. *Kappa Delta Pi Record, 49*(3), 113–15.

Dixon, A. D., Royal, C., & Henry, Jr, K. L. (2014). School reform and school choice. In H. R. Milner IV & K. Lomotey (Eds.), *Handbook of urban education* (pp. 474–503). New York, NY: Routledge.

Howe, K. Eisehart, M., & Betebenner, D. (2001). School choice crucible: A case study of Boulder Valley. *Phi Delta Kappan, 83*(2), 137–46.

Hubard, K. (2014). Missouri's school transfer law: Not a Hancock violation but a mere bandage on wounded districts. *Missouri Law Review, 79*(3), 783–806.

Jacobs, R. T. (2011). An experiment to test the feasibility of a web-based questionnaire of teachers. *Evaluation Review, 35*(1), 40–70.

Jimerson, L. (2002). Interdistrict open enrollment: the benign choice? *Clearing House, 76*(1), 16.

Lavery, L., Witte, J. F., & Carlson, D. (2012). The determinants of interdistrict open enrollment flows: Evidence from two states. *Educational Evaluation and Policy Analysis*, 33(1), 76-94.

Lavery, L., & Carlson, D. (2015). Dynamic participation in interdistrict open enrollment. *Educational Policy, 29*(5), 746–79.

Ledwith, V. (2010). The influence of open enrollment on scholastic achievement among public school students in Los Angeles. *American Journal of Education, 116*(2), 243–62.

Malugade, L. (2014). Open enrollment: What's in the best interest of Wisconsin students, families, and public schools? *Marquette Law Review*, 97(3), 813-851.

Miron, G., Horvitz, B., & Gulosino, C. (2013). *Virtual schools in the U.S. 2013: Politics, performance, policy, and research evidence* (pp. 1–16) (United States, National Education Policy Center). Boulder, CO: NEPC. http://nepc.colorado.edu/files/nepc-virtual-2013-section-1-2.pdf.

Moe, T. M. (2008). Beyond the free market: The structure of school choice. *Brigham Young University Law Review, 2008*(2), 557–92.

Ni, Y. (2012). Teacher working conditions in charter schools and traditional public schools: A comparative study. *Teachers College Record, 114*(3), 1–26.

Reback, R. (2008). Teaching to the rating: School accountability and the distribution of student achievement. *Journal of Public Economics, 92*(5-6), 1394–415.

Appendix I

Social Justice Guidance and Resources for Teachers and Administrators

ARTICLES

Bemak, F., & Chi-Ying Chung, R. (2008, summer). New professional roles and advocacy strategies for school counselors: A multicultural/social justice perspective to move beyond the nice counselor syndrome. *Journal of Counseling & Development, 86,* 372–82. http://edresearch.yolasite.com/resources/BemakChung.pdf.

David, S., & Hoppenstedt, D. (2014). Social justice: One district's comprehensive approach to increasing student engagement. *Michigan Association of School Administrators.* http://www.gomasa.org /news/social-justice-one-district-s-comprehensive-approach-increasing-student-engagement.

Dupree, M. (2015, May 4). Here's what white teachers tend to do with gifted black students; it's appalling. *Financial Juneteenth.* http://financialjuneteenth.com/heres-what-white-teachers-tend-to-do-with-gifted-black-students-its-appalling/.

Ford, D. Y., & Toldson, I. A. Study on black, hispanic children in special ed: Wrong, regressive. (2015, July 5). *Diverse: Issues in higher education.* http://diverseeducation.com/article/76088/.

Green, E. J., McCollum, V. C., & Hays, D. G. (2008). Teaching advocacy counseling: A social justice paradigm of awareness, knowledge, and skills. *Journal for Social Action in Counseling and Psychology, 1*(2), 14–29. http://www.psysr.org/about/pubs_ resources/jsacp/Green-V1N2-08.pdf.

ACTIVITIES/INFORMATION (TOPICAL)

Differential Discipline Based on Race

Chiles, N. (2015, April 16). Stanford researchers unveil racial stereotypes that lead teachers to discipline black students more severely. *Atlanta Black Star.* http://atlantablackstar.com/2015/04/16/stanford-researchers-unveil-racial-stereotypes-that-lead-teachers-to-discipline-black-students-more-severely/.

Dobuzinskis, A. (2015, April 15). U.S. study finds teacher bias in discipline toward black students. *Reuters*. http://www.reuters.com/article/2015/04/16/us-usa-race-schooldiscipline-idUSKBN0N701C20150416.

Rowe, C. (2015, June 23). Race dramatically skews discipline, even in elementary school. *The Seattle Times*. http://www.seattletimes.com/education-lab/race-dramatically-skews-discipline-even-in-elementary-school/.

U.S. Department of Education. (2015, July). *Educators gather at the white house to rethink school discipline*. http://www.ed.gov/news/press-releases/educators-gather-white-house-rethink-school-discipline.

U.S. Department of Education Office for Civil Rights. (2014, March). *Civil rights data collection, data snapshot: school discipline*. http://ocrdata.ed.gov/Downloads/CRDC-School-Discipline-Snapshot.pdf.

White Privilege

Diangelo, R. (2015, April 9) White fragility: Why it's so hard to talk to white people about tacism. *The Good Men Project*. http://goodmenproject.com /featured-content/white-fragility-why-its-so-hard-to-talk-to-white-people-about-racism-twlm/.

Institute for Humane Education (2012, May 21). 13 resources for teaching about white privilege. *Institute for Humane Education*. http://humaneeducation.org/blog/2012/05/21/13-resources-for-teaching-about-white-privilege/.

LaBouvier C. (n.d.). I racist. *Those people*. https://thsppl.com/i-racist-538512462265.

Marusic, K. (2015, June 22). 9 ways you can use your white privilege for good. *MTV News* . http://www.mtv.com/news/2187137/white-people-documentary-privilege-for-good/.

McIntosh, P. (1988). White privilege: Unpacking the invisible knapsack. http://www.deanza.edu/faculty/lewisjulie/White%20Priviledge%20Unpacking%20the%20Invisible %20Knapsack.pdf.

Pang, E. (2015, July 6). Wondering what "privilege" is? This video has some answers for you. *Huffington Post*. http://www.huffingtonpost.ca /2015/07/06/what-is-privilege_n_7737466.html.

Sehgal, P. (2015, July 14). How "privilege" became a provocation. *The New York Times*. http://www.nytimes.com/2015/07/19/magazine/how-privilege-became-a-provocation.html?_r=0.

Southern Poverty Law Center. (2012). Confronting white privilege. *Teaching tolerance*. http://www.tolerance.org/magazine/number-42-fall-2012/feature/ confronting-white-privilege.

Microaggressions

Kaskan, E. R., & Ho, I. K. (2014, November). Microaggressions and female athletes.*Sex Roles*, *20*. http://link.springer.com/article/10.1007%2Fs11199-014-0425-1#page-1.

Pérez Huber, L., & Solorzano, D. G. (2015). Racial microaggressions as atool for critical race research. *Race Ethnicity and Education*, *18*(3), 297–320. http://dx.doi.org/10.1080/ 13613324.2014.994173.

Sue, D. W. (2010). *Microaggressions in everyday life: Race, gender, and sexual orientation*. Hoboken, NJ: John Wiley & Sons.

Sue, D. W. (2010, October). Racial microaggressions in everyday life. Is subtle bias harmless? *Psychology Today*.https://www.psychologytoday.com/blog/microaggressions-in-everyday-life/201010/racial-microaggressions-in-everyday-life.

Sue, D. W., Capodilupo, C. M., Torino, G. C., Bucceri, J. M., Holder, A. M. D., Nadal, K. L., & Esquilin, M. (2007). Racial microaggressions in everyday life: Implications for clinical practice. *American Psychologist*, *62*(4), 271–86. http://www.consumerstar.org/resources/pdf/racialmicroaggressions.pdf.

The Microaggression Project. (n.d.). Microaggressions: Power, privilege, and everyday life. http://www.microaggressions.com/.

N.A. (n.d.). *Examples of racial microaggressions*. http://www.uwsp.edu/acadaff/ NewFacultyResources/NFSRacialMicroaggressions_Table.pdf.

Vega, T. (2014, March 21). Students see many slights as racial "microaggressions." *The New York Times*. http://www.nytimes.com/2014/03/22/us/as-diversity-increases-slights-get-subtler-but-still-sting.html?_r=0.
[See *I too am Harvard* in video section.]

CURRICULUM

Anti-defamation league. (2015). *Social justice poetry*. http://www.adl.org/assets/pdf/education-outreach/social-justice-poetry.pdf.
Ciardiello, A. V. (2010). "Talking walls": Presenting a case for social justice poetry in literacy education. *The Reading Teacher, 63*(6), 464–73. http://www.aiisf.org/pdf/TalkingWalls.pdf.
Deshmukh Towert, I. Oliveri, R., & Gidney, C. L. (2007). Peer-led professional development for equity and diversity: A report for teachers and administrators based on findings from the SEED Project (Seeking Educational Equity and Diversity). *Schott Foundation for Public Education.* Retrieved from http://www.schottfoundation.org/drupal/publications/Seed%20Schott%20Report%20Final%20Version.pdf .
Greenberg, J. (2015, July 10). Curriculum for white Americans to educate themselves on race and racism–from Ferguson to Charleston. *Citizenship & Social Justice.* http://citizenshipandsocialjustice.com/2015/07/10/curriculum-for-white-americans-to-educate-themselves-on-race-and-racism/.

ORGANIZATIONS

Edchange: Bringing equitable and just schools, communities, and organizations through transformative action. http://www.edchange.org/.
National Association for Multicultural Education
National Alliance for Partnerships in Equity
Southern Poverty Law Center (Teaching Tolerance)

RESOURCES

New York Department of Education. (n.d.). Respect for all: Useful links for teachers and school administrators. http://schools.nyc.gov/RulesPolicies/RespectforAll/EducatorResources/default.htm.
Teaching Tolerance. (n.d.). *Family and community engagement.* http://www.tolerance.org/publication/family-and-community-engagement.
Teaching Tolerance. (n.d.). The southern poverty law center. http://www.tolerance.org/?source=redirect&url=teachingtolerance.
U.S. Department of Education. (2014, January). *Guiding principals: A resource guide for improving school climate and discipline.* http://www2.ed.gov/policy/gen/guid/school-discipline/guiding-principles.pdf.
U.S. Office for Civil Rights. (2011, April 4). *Dear colleague letter: Sexual violence.* http://www2.ed.gov/about/offices/list/ocr/letters/colleague-201104.pdf.
U.S. Office for Civil Rights. (2012, October 26). *Dear colleague letter: Harassment and bullying.* http://www2.ed.gov/about/offices/list/ocr/letters/colleague-201010.pdf.
U.S. Office for Civil Rights. (2014, January 8). *Dear colleague letter: Nondiscriminatory Administration of School Discipline.* http://www2.ed.gov/about/offices/list/ocr/letters/colleague-201401-title-vi.pdf.
U.S. Office for Civil Rights. (2015, April 24). *Dear colleague letter: Title IX coordinators.* http://www2.ed.gov/about/offices/list/ocr/letters/colleague-201504-title-ix-coordinators.pdf.

SIMULATIONS

Harvard Implicit Bias Tests: https://implicit.harvard.edu/implicit/ takeatest.html.

Crossing the Line, Facilitation Guidelines: http://freechild.org/Firestarter/ CrossingTheLine.htm.

BaFa BaFa: Can be found at http://www.simulationtrainingsystems.com/ corporate/products/bafa-bafa/ .

The Dance of Structural Inequality: http://www.cirtl.net/files/ ActionsYouCanTake_DanceofStructuralInequality_FacilitationGuidelines. pdf (see video example below).

VIDEOS

Bailey, M. (2014). The danger of hiding who you are. *Ted Talks.* https://www.ted.com/talks/ morgana_bailey_the_danger_of_hiding_who_you_are.

Burns, J. (2010). A message to gay teens: It gets better. *Ted Talks.* https://www.ted.com/talks/ joel_burns_tells_gay_teens_it_gets_better.

Cliatt-Wayman, L. (2015). How to fix a broken school? Lead fearlessly, love hard. *Ted Talks.* http://www.spotlightonpoverty.org/news.aspx?id=cbacd1e2-947c4e77-9cc8-7beaae2e9aeb.

Choonara, E. (2014). What is intersectionality? *You Tube.* https://www.youtube.com/watch?v= aIoy9G3KnLE.

Collins, P. H. (2013). Intersectionality. *C-Span.* http://www.cspan.org/video/?c4289652/ intersectionality.

The dance of structural inequality video. https://www.youtube.com/watch?v=hD5f8GuNuGQ.

Fukishima, A. (2013). Intersectionality matters: Alisha Fukishima at Tedx Whitman College. *You Tube.* https://www.youtube.com/watch?v=aIoy9G3KnLE.

Gebreyes, R. (2015, June, 1). How misperceptions of "aggressive" black female behavior lead to tough punishments for young girls. *Huffington Post.* http://www.huffingtonpost.com/ 2015/06/01/punishments-black-girls-aggressive-behavior_n_7484356.html.

I too am Harvard. http://itooamharvard.tumblr.com/.

Jackson, S. (2010). Intersection analysis of Race, class, and education. *YouTube.* https://www. youtube.com/watch?v=InhCz3_Csr0.

Jackson, Y. (n.d.). Challenging myths of educating low-income children. *Spotlight on poverty and opportunity: The source for news, ideas, and actions.* https://www.ted.com/talks/linda_ cliatt_wayman_how_to_fix_a_broken_school_lead_fearlessly_love_hard.

Jane Eliot: Blue eyes/brown eyes. https://www.youtube.com/watch?v=uQAmdZvKf6M.

Jane Eliot: How racist are you? https://www.youtube.com/watch?v=XAv8JA_9uKI.

Jane Eliot: Oprah. http://www.huffingtonpost.com/2015/01/02/jane-elliott-race-experiment-oprah-show_n_6396980.html.

Katz, J. (2012). *Violence against women: It's a men's issue.* https://www.ted.com/talks/ jackson_katz_violence_against_women_it_s_a_men_s_issue.

The linguistics of AAVE. (2015). https://www.youtube.com/watch?v=pkzVOXKXfQk.

PBS Video. (2012). Does being poor mean you will stay poor? *Public Broadcasting System.* http://video.pbs.org/video/2298446394/.

PBS Video. (2015). Why poverty? *Public Broadcasting System.* http://video.pbs.org/program/ why-poverty/.

Pilloton, E. (2010). Teaching design for change. *Ted Talks.* https://www.ted.com/talks/emily_ pilloton_teaching_design_for_change.

Porter, T. (2010). *A call to men.* https://www.ted.com/talks/tony_porter_a_call_to_men.

Rakestraw, M. (2014). 9 videos for exploring gender stereotypes and gender roles. *The Institute for Humane Education Blog.* http://humaneeducation.org/blog/2014/06/30/9-videos-exploring-gender-stereotypes gender-roles/.

The Representation Project (n.d.). The mask you live in. http://therepresentationproject.org/films/the-mask-you-live-in/.

Richen, Y. (2014). What the gay rights movement learned from the civil rights movement. *Ted Talks.* https://www.ted.com/talks/zimchallenge.

Teaching Channel. (2015). Closing the gender gap in STEM education. *Teaching Channel.* https://www.teachingchannel.org/videos/stem-gender-gap-ced.

TVSBSC. (2012). Intersectionality of race and gender: A framework for learning, dialogue, and change. *You Tube.* https://www.youtube.com/watch?v=66XEglI-EEo.

Weill, J. (2015). Spotlight webcast: FRAC reports on the success of school breakfast. *Spotlight on Poverty and Opportunity: The Source for News, Ideas, and Actions.* http://www.spotlightonpoverty.org/news.aspx?id=4144dc38-980b-4d1b 9256-a198c30e936a.

Zimbardo, P. (2011). The demise of guys? *Ted Talks.* https://www.ted.com/talks/zimchallenge.

WEBSITES

Adwar, C. (2014, March 26). Amazing new tool lets you see the racial disparities at your old high school. *Business Insider Education.* http://www.businessinsider.com/education-department-releases-school-equity-data-2014-3.

Benn, M. (2014). The education gender gap is bas for girls as well as boys. *The Guardian.* http://www.theguardian.com/commentisfree/2014/jan/31/education-gender-gap-girlsschools-university.

Boyd, N. (2015). Improving equality in education. *Study.com.* http://study.com/academy/lesson/improving-gender-equality-in-education.html.

Chapman, A. (2015). Gender bias in education. EdChange.org. http://www.edchange.org/multicultural/papers/genderbias.html.

Child Fund International. (2015). The effects of poverty in the United States. https://www.childfund.org/Poverty-and-Education-in-the-US/.

Coley, R. J., & Baker, B. (2013). Poverty and education: Finding the way forward. Education Testing Service. https://www.ets.org/s/research/pdf/poverty_and_education_report.pdf.

Columbia University. (2014). National Center for Children in Poverty. http://www.nccp.org.

DoSomething.org. (n.d.). 11 facts about education and poverty in America. https://www.dosomething.org/facts/11-facts-about-education-and-poverty-america.

Education World. (n.d.). States step up efforts to reduce school segregation. *Education World.* http://www.educationworld.com/a_admin/admin/admin154.shtml.

The Fenway Institute. (2015). The National LGBT Health Education Center. http://www.lgbthealtheducation.org/training/learning-modules/.

Galupo, M. P. (2014). Advancing diversity through a framework of intersectionality: inclusion of LGBT issues in higher education. *Association of American Colleges and Universities.* http://www.diversityweb.org/digest/vol10no2/galupo.cfm.

Gay, Lesbian, & Straight Education Network. http://www.glsen.org.

Hurst, M. (2015). Gender differences in the classroom: Physical, cognitive, & behavioral. *Study.com.* http://study.com/academy/lesson/gender-differences-in-the-classroom-physical-cognitive-behavioral.html.

Intergroup Resources. (2012). Intersectionality. *Intergroup Resources.* http://www.intergroupresources.com/intersectionality/.

Jensen, E. (2009). Teaching with poverty in mind. *ASCD.* http://www.ascd.org/publications/books/109074/chapters/How-Poverty-Affects-Behavior-and-Academic-Performance.aspx.

National Education Association. (2015). Research spotlight on single-gender education. http://www.nea.org/tools/17061.htm.

Poverty USA. (n.d.). Learn about the state of poverty. *United States Conference of Bishops.* http://www.povertyusa.org/the-state-of-poverty/.

Salera, B. (2014). Intersectionality in the classroom: My experience teaching at the crossroads of ethnicity and gender. *Hybrid Pedagogy.* http://www.hybridpedagogy.com/journal/intersectionality-classroom-experience-teaching-crossroads-ethnicity-gender/.

Save Our Schools. (2014). A nation's priority: Poverty and/or the children? http://saveourschoolsmarch.org/issues/poverty-and-the-effect-on-education/.

Stanberry, K. (2015). Single-sex education: The pros and cons. *Great Kids.* http://www.greatschools.org/gk/articles/single-sex-education-the pros-and-cons/.

Teaching Tolerance. (2013). Best practices. Creating an LGBT-inclusive climate: A teaching tolerance guide for school leaders. *Southern Poverty Law Center.* http://www.tolerance.org/sites/default/files/general/LGBT%20Best%20Practices_0.pdf.

United Nations Educational, Scientific and Cultural Organization. (2015). Gender equality in education. http://www.unesco.org/new/en/education/themes/leading-the-internationalagenda/gender-and-education/.

Appendix II

Multicultural Resources for Teachers and Administrators

TERMS AND NOTIONS IN THE PROGRESSION OF OUR THINKING ABOUT RACE AND CULTURE

For most of the history of American education, students of color and students in poverty were viewed as culturally deprived, and thus not capable of achieving on par with their white, middle-class counterparts. Instead, they were provided with tracked classes and watered-down curriculums, less qualified or capable teachers, and fewer academic resources. According to Paris (2012), "Deficit approaches to teaching and learning, firmly in place prior to and during the 1960s and 1970s, viewed the languages, literacies, and cultural ways of being of many students and communities of color as deficiencies to be overcome in learning the demanded and legitimized dominant language, literacy, and cultural ways of schooling" (p. 93). One of the goals of these approaches was to eradicate the home cultures and literacy practices that many students brought to school from their homes and communities in order to replace them with what were considered to be correct, proper, and superior practices (Morris & Monroe, 2009; Paris, 2012).

Lee (2003) argues that although we have progressed beyond the pejorative terms of "culturally deprived" and "culturally disadvantaged," we still have terms such as "inner-city," "at-risk" (p. 3), and "urban" that are codes for those not classified as white.

According to Lee (2003), "the European-American middle class is consistently used as the point of reference from which to compare cultural practices with other national and international ethnic groups" (p. 3). Although the terms "culturally deprived" and "culturally disadvantaged" are used with less frequency within the current educational milieu, the implications are still with us.

Various scholars have outlined the progression of how educators (most of whom historically have been white) think about and talk about race and culture within education. To summarize:

- *Culturally deprived* (Lee, 2003) is the notion that people of color do not have a meaningful culture, or that non-white culture is somehow "less than."
- *Deficit approaches* (Paris, 2012), which dominated the twentieth century, view children and the cultures of which they are a part through negative comparisons with white, middle-class culture, instead of viewing cultures on their own terms (e.g., Indian boarding schools).
- *Difference approaches* (Paris, 2012) began to develop in the 1970s and 1980s as a progression to viewing language/culture/community as "equal to, but different from" in-school knowledge.
- *Resource pedagogies* (Moll & Gonzalez, 1994) involve viewing communities of color as resources to explore; for example, Moll and Gonzalez's (1994) conception of "funds of knowledge," which refers to "historically accumulated and culturally developed bodies of knowledge and skills essential for household or individual functioning and well-being" (p. 133).
- *Third space* (Gutierrez, 2008) addresses an imagined future, where "curriculum and its pedagogy. . . grounded in the historical and current particulars of students' everyday lives, while at the same time oriented toward an imagined possible future" (p. 154). According to Paris (2012), this third space requires that "teaching and learning is not simply about building bridges for students between the often disparate knowledges of home, community, and school spaces but that teachers and students must bring together and extend the various activities and practices of these domains in a forward-looking third space" (p. 94).
- *Critical Race Theory* (Bell, 1992), Ladson-Billings (2012) argues that racism is a normative aspect of U.S. society. In their analysis of CRT, DeCuir and Dixson (2004) argue that counter-narratives are crucial in dismantling myths and stereotypes of students of color "by telling their stories in their own words, their counter-narratives allow them to contradict the Othering process, and, thus, challenge the privileged discourses that are often found at elite, predominantly White, independent schools" (p. 27). Critical Race Theory also necessitates a critique of Whiteness, which is made virtually impossible by the liberal ideology of colorblindness.
- *Culturally relevant pedagogy* (Ladson-Billings, 1995) Ladson-Billings advocated for a culturally relevant pedagogy that would do three things: "produce students who can achieve academically, produce students who

demonstrate cultural competence, and develop students who can both understand and critique the existing social order" (p. 474). According to Paris (2012), Ladson-Billings's conception of a culturally relevant pedagogy involves "supporting students in maintaining their community and heritage ways with language and other cultural practices in the process of gaining access to dominant ones. In her third tenet, Ladson-Billings also called for the development of an explicitly critical and praxis-oriented stance in students" (p. 94).

- *Critical multiculturalism* (Castro, 2010) "Critical multiculturalism strives to bring about the transformation of society to accomplish the goals of social justice by confronting and disrupting institutions and the structures of power that maintain disparities across race, class, and gender" (p. 199).
- *Culturally sustaining pedagogy* (Paris, 2012) Paris critiques Ladson-Billings's use of the term "relevance" as being inadequate. Instead, he offers the term "culturally sustaining pedagogy," which "requires that our pedagogies be more than responsive of or relevant to the cultural experiences and practices of young people—it requires that they support young people in sustaining the cultural and linguistic competence of their communities while simultaneously offering access to dominant cultural competence" (p. 95).

REFERENCES

Bell, D. (1992). Racial realism. *Connecticut Law Review, 24*(2), 363–79.

Castro, A. J. (2010). Themes in the research on preservice teachers' views of cultural diversity: Implications for researching millennial preservice teachers. *Educational Researcher, 39*(3), 198–210.

DeCuir, J. T., & Dixson, A. D. (2004). "So when it comes out, they aren't that surprised that it is there": Using critical race theory as a tool of analysis of race and racism in education. *Educational Researcher, 33*(5), 26–31.

Gutierrez, K. (2008). Developing a sociocritical literacy in the third space. *Reading Research Quarterly, 43*, 148–64.

Ladson-Billings, G. (2012). Through a glass darkly: The persistence of race in education research and scholarship. *Educational Researcher, 41*(4), 115–20.

Ladson-Billings, G., & Tate, E. (1995). Toward a critical race theory of education. *Teachers College Record, 97*(1), 47–67.

Lee, C. D. (2003). Why we need to re-think race and ethnicity in educational research. *Educational Researcher, 32*(5), 3–5.

Moll, L., & Gonzalez, N. (1994). Lessons from research with language minority children. *Journal of Reading Behavior, 26*(4), 23–41.

Morris, J. E., & Monroe, C. R. (2009). Why study the U.S. south? The nexus of race and place in investigating black student achievement. *Educational Researcher, 38*(1), 21–36.

Paris, D. (2012). Culturally sustaining pedagogy: A needed change in stance, terminology, and practice. *Educational Researcher, 41*(3), 93–97.

ARTICLES

Bemak, F. & Chi-Ying Chung, R. (2008, summer). New professional roles and advocacy strategies for school counselors: A multicultural/social justice perspective to move beyond the nice counselor syndrome. *Journal of Counseling & Development, 86*, 372–82. http://edresearch.yolasite.com/resources/BemakChung.pdf.

Chesler, M. (2003). Teaching well in the diverse/multicultural classroom. http://www.aahea.org/articles/sociology.htm.

Chou, H. (2007, Summer). Multicultural teacher education: Toward a culturally responsive pedagogy. *Essays in Education, 21*, 139–62. http://www.usca.edu/essays/vol212007/chourevised.pdf.

Gorski, P. (n.d.). Stages of multicultural school transformation. *ED change*. http://www.edchange.org/multicultural/resources/school_transformation.html.

ACTIVITIES AND INFORMATION

Talking about Race

Hannah-Jones, N. (2015, June 29), What Abigail Fisher's affirmative action case is really about. *Pro publica*. http://www.rawstory.com/2015/07/what-abigail-fishers-affirmative-action-case-is-really-about/.

Johnson, C. (2015, June 24). Bryan Stevenson on Charleston and our real problem with race. *The Marshall Project*. https://www.themarshallproject.org/2015/06/24/bryan-stevenson-on-charleston-and-our-real-problem-with-race.

Lurie, J. (2015, April 17). Just how racist are schoolteachers? *Mother Jones*. http://www.motherjones.com/kevin-drum/2015/04/teachers-racism-bias-stanford.

Milner, H. R. (2015, July 1). Educators shouldn't avoid the tough conversations. *Education Week*. http://blogs.edweek.org/edweek/op_education/2015/07/educators_shouldnt_avoid_the_tough_conversations.html.

Milner, H. R. (2015, July 1). Getting race and poverty right in education. *Diverse Issues in Higher Education*. http://diverseeducation.com/article/76058/.

Curriculum

Colorin Colorado. (n.d.). Multicultural resources for the classroom. http://www.colorincolorado.org/web_resources/by_topic/multicultural_resources_for_classroom/.

Deshmukh Towert, I. Oliveri, R., & Gidney, C. L. (2007). Peer-led professional development for equity and diversity: A report for teachers and administrators based on findings from the SEED Project (Seeking Educational Equity and Diversity). *Schott Foundation for Public Education*. Retrieved from http://www.schottfoundation.org/drupal/publications/Seed%20Schott%20Report%20Final%20Version.pdf.

Kea, C., Campbell-Whatley, G. D., & Richards, H. V. (2006). Becoming culturally responsive educators: Rethinking teacher education pedagogy. *National Center for Culturally Responsive Educational Systems: Education for all*. http://www.nccrest.org/Briefs/Teacher_Ed_Brief.pdf.

Loyola University. (n.d.). Curriculum resources on the Internet: Multicultural resources. *Loyola University*. http://libguides.luc.edu/c.php?g=49783&p=320646.

Organizations

Edchange: Bringing equitable and just schools, communities, and organizations through transformative action: http://www.edchange.org/.

National Alliance for Partners in Equity (NAPE): http://www.napequity.org/.

The National Association for Multicultural Education (NAME): http://www.nameorg.org/.
Southern Poverty Law Center: https://www.splcenter.org/.
Teaching Tolerance: http://www.tolerance.org/.

Resources

Center for Research on learning and teaching. (n.d.). Diversity and inclusion. *The University of Michigan*. http://www.crlt.umich.edu/multicultural-teaching.
The National Association for Multicultural Education. (n.d.). http://www.nameorg.org/.
National Education Association. (2015). *Resources for addressing multicultural and diversity issues in your classroom: Books, websites and other resources help you learn about multicultural and diversity issues. NEA*. http://www.nea.org/tools/resources-addressing-multicultural-diversity-issues-in-your-classroom.htm.
National MultiCultural Institute. (n.d.). http://www.nmci.org/.
Teachers: Where Teachers Come First. (n.d.). Multiculturalism and diversity. Scholastic. http://www.scholastic.com/teachers/lesson-plan/multiculturalism-and-diversity.
Teaching Tolerance. (n.d.). *Family and community engagement*. http://www.tolerance.org/publication/family-and-community-engagement.
Teaching Tolerance. (n.d.). The Southern Poverty Law Center. http://www.tolerance.org/?source=redirect&url=teachingtolerance.

Simulations

Harvard Implicit Bias Tests: https://implicit.harvard.edu/implicit/takeatest.html.
Crossing the Line, Facilitation Guidelines: http://freechild.org/Firestarter/CrossingTheLine.htm.
BaFa BaFa: http://www.simulationtrainingsystems.com/corporate/products/bafa-bafa/.
The Dance of Structural Inequality: http://www.cirtl.net/files/ActionsYouCanTake_DanceofStructuralInequality_FacilitationGuidelines.pdf.

Videos

The Dance of Structural Inequality video. https://www.youtube.com/watch?v=hD5f8GuNuGQ.
Jane Eliot: Blue eyes/brown eyes. https://www.youtube.com/watch?v=uQAmdZvKf6M.
Jane Eliot: How racist are you? https://www.youtube.com/watch?v=XAv8JA_9uKI.
Jane Eliot: Oprah. http://www.huffingtonpost.com/2015/01/02/jane-elliott-race-experiment-oprah-show_n_6396980.html.

Websites

Brown, S. (2002, Fall). In it together: Teacher networks support multicultural education. *The Notebook*. http://thenotebook.org/fall-2002/021465/it-together-teacher-networks-support-multicultural-education.

Walsh, B. (2015, January 26). Getting to excellence with equity: Ron Ferguson talks about opportunity, achievement, and raising the bar for all students. *Usable knowledge: Connecting research to practice*. http://www.gse.harvard.edu/news/uk/15/01/getting-excellence-equity.

FOR FURTHER READING

Adams, M., Bell, L. E., & Griffin, P. (Eds.). (1997). *Teaching for diversity and social justice.* New York, NY: Routledge.

Adams, M., Blumenfeld, R, Castaneda, Hackman, H.W., Peters, M.L., & Zuniga (Eds.). (2000). *Readings for diversity and social justice; Sexism, anti-Semitism, heterosexism, classism and ableism: An anthology on racism* (2nd Ed). New York, NY: Routledge.

Adams, V. (2013). *Markets of sorrow, labors of faith: New Orleans in the wake of Katrina.* Durham, NC: Duke University Press.

Akiba, M. (2011). Identifying program characteristics for preparing pre-service teachers for diversity. *Teachers College Record, 113*(3), 658–97.

Allport, G. W. (1954). *The nature of prejudice.* Reading, MA: Addison-Wesley.

Artiles, A. J. (2011). Toward an interdisciplinary understanding of educational equity and difference: The case of the racialization of ability. *Educational Researcher, 40*(9), 431–45.

Asanti, M. (1988). *Afrocentricity: The theory of social change.* Trenton, NJ: African World Press.

Asher, N. (2007). Made in the (multicultural) U.S.A.: Unpacking tensions of race, culture, gender, and sexuality in education. *Educational Researcher, 36*(2), 65–73.

Baker, G. C. (1988). Recognition of our culturally pluralistic society and multicultural education in our schools. *Education and Society, 1*(1), 23–28.

Banks, J. A. (1988). *Multicultural education: Theory and practice.* Boston: Allyn and Bacon.

Banks, J. A. (2001). Citizenship education and diversity: Implications for teacher education. *Journal of Teacher Education, 52*(1), 5–16.

Banks, J. A. (2006). *Cultural diversity and education: Foundations, curriculum and teaching* (4th ed.). Boston, MA: Allyn and Bacon Pearson.

Banks, J. A. (2006). *Race, culture, and education: The selected works of James A. Banks.* New York, NY: Routledge.

Banks, J. A. (2007). *Educating citizens in a multicultural society* (2nd ed.). New York, NY: Teachers College Press.

Banks, J. A. (2009). *Teaching strategies for ethnic studies* (8th ed.). Boston, MA: Pearson Allyn and Bacon.

Banks, J. A., & McGee Banks, C. A. (1998). *Teaching strategies for the social studies: Decision-making and citizen action* (5th ed.). New York, NY: Longman.

Bartolome, L. I. (1994). Beyond the methods fetish: Towards a humanizing pedagogy. *Harvard Educational Review, 64*(2), 172–94.

Bell, D. (1992). Racial realism. *Connecticut Law Review, 24*(2), 363–79.

Biklen, R. (1985). *The complete school: Integrating special and regular education.* New York, NY: Columbia University Press.

Blanchett, W. J. (2006). Disproportionate representation of African American students in special education: Acknowledging the role of white privilege and racism. *Educational Researcher, 35*(6), 24–28.

Bogdan, R. (1986). *Special education: Research and trends.* Elmsford, NY: Pergannon.

Bolotin Joseph, P., Luster Bravmann, S., Windschitl, M. A., Mikel, E. R., & Stewart Green, N. (2000). *Cultures of curriculum.* Mahwah, NJ: Lawrence Erlbaum Associates, Publishers.

Brown, P., Reay, D., & Vincent, C. (2013). Education and social mobility. *British Journal of Sociology of Education, 34*(5-6), 637–43.

Bullivant, B. (1989). *Multicultural education: Issues and perspectives.* Boston: Allyn and Bacon.

Carter Andrews, D. J. (2012). Black achievers' experiences with racial spotlighting and ignoring in a predominantly white high school. *Teachers College Record, 114*(10), 1–46.

Casella, R. (2003, November). Punishing dangerousness through preventive detention: Illustrating the institutional link between school and prison. *New Directions for Youth Development. Special Issue: Deconstructing the School-to-Prison Pipeline, 99,* 55–70.

Castro, A. J. (2010). Themes in the research on preservice teachers' views of cultural diversity: Implications for researching millennial preservice teachers. *Educational Researcher, 39*(3), 198–210.

Center for Evidence-Based Crime Policy. (2014). *Broken windows policing*. George Mason University. http://cebcp.org/evidence-based-policing/what-works-in-policing/research-evidence-review/broken-windows-policing/.

Chapman, T. K. (2007). Interrogating classroom relationships and events: Using portraiture and critical race theory in education research. *Educational Researcher, 36*(3), 156–62.

Chappell, M. (2010). *The war on welfare: Family, poverty, and politics in modern America.* Philadelphia, PA: The University of Pennsylvania Press.

Charity Hudley, A. H., & Mallinson, C. (2012). *Understanding English language variation in U.S. schools.* New York, NY: Teachers College Press.

Clinchy, E., & Kolb, F. (1989). *Planning for schools of choice: Achieving equity and excellence.* Andover, MA: Network, Inc.

Cortes, C. (2000). *The children are watching: How the media teach about diversity.* New York, NY: Teachers College Press.

Costa, M. D., & James, S. (1975). *The power of women and the subversion of the community.* London, UK: Falling Wall Press.

Counts, G. (1932). *Dare the school build a new social order?* Carbondale, IL: Southern Illinois University Press.

Daniels, H. A. (1990). *Not only English: Affirming America's multilingual heritage.* Urbana, IL: National Council of Teachers of English.

DeCuir, J. T., & Dixson, A. D. (2004). "So when it comes out, they aren't that surprised that it is there": Using critical race theory as a tool of analysis of race and racism in education. *Educational Researcher, 33*(5), 26–31.

Delpit, L. (2003). Educators as "seed people": Growing a new future. *Educational Leadership, 7*(32), 14–21.

Delpit, L. (1995). *Other people's children: Cultural conflict in the classroom.* New York, NY: The New Press.

Dewey, J. (1916). *Democracy and education.* New York, NY: Macmillan.

DiAngelo, R. (2012). Nothing to add: The role of white silence in racial discussions. *Journal of Understanding and Dismantling Privilege, 2*(2), 1–17.

Dover, A. G. (2013). Getting "up to code": Preparing for and confronting challenges when teaching for social justice in standards-based classrooms. *Action in Teacher Education, 35*(2), 89–102.

Fagan, J., & Davies, G. (2000). Street stops and broken windows: Terry, race, and disorder in New York City. *Fordham Urban Law Journal, 28*(3), 457–504.

Farrington, C. A. (2014). *Failing at school: Lessons for redesigning urban high schools.* New York, NY: Teachers College Press.

Feistritzer, C. E. (2011, July). *Profiles of Teachers in the U.S. 2011.* National Center for Education Information. pot2011final-blog.pdf.

Fine, M. (1991). *Framing dropouts: Notes on the politics of an urban high school.* Albany, NY: State University of New York Press.

Fraschl, M. & Sprung, B. (1986). *Building community: A manual exploring issues of women and disabilities.* Women and Disabilities Awareness Project, Equity Concepts, Inc.

Fraser, N., & Linda G. (1994). A genealogy of dependency: Tracing a keyword of the U.S. welfare state. *Signs, 19*(2), 309–36.

Freire, P. (1974). *Pedagogy of the oppressed.* New York, NY: Seabury Press.

Furnin, T. L. (2009). *Combating hatred: Educators leading the way.* Lanham, MD: Rowman & Littlefield.

Gaines, L. K., & Miller, L. E. (2014). *Criminal justice in action: The core* (7th ed.). Belmont, CA: Wadsworth.

Gay, G. (2000). *Culturally responsive teaching: Theory, research and practice.* New York, NY: Teachers College Press.

Gay, G., & Howard, T. (2000). Multicultural teacher education for the 21st century. *The Teacher Educator, 36*(1), 1–16.

Ginsberg, A. E. (2012). *Embracing risk in urban education: Curiosity, creativity, and courage in the era of "no excuses" and relay race reform.* Lanham, MD: Rowman & Littlefield.

Giroux, H. A., & McLaren. (1989). *Critical pedagogy, the state, and cultural struggles.* Albany, NY: The State University of New York.

Goff, P. A., Jackson, M. C., Di Leone, B. A., L., Culotta, C. M., & DiTomasso, N. A. (2014). The essence of innocence: Consequences of dehumanizing black children. *Journal of Personality and Social Psychology, 106*(4), 526–45. https://www.apa.org/pubs/journals/releases/psp-a0035663.pdf.

Goldberg, G. S., & Collins, S. D. (2001). *Washington's new poor law: Welfare reform and the roads not taken—1935 to the present.* New York, NY: Apex Press.

Good, T. L., & Brophy, J. E.. (1987). *Looking in classrooms.* (4th ed.). New York: Harper and Row.

Gordon, A. (1979). *The nature of prejudice.* Cambridge, MA: Addison-Wesley.

Gordon, L. (1994). *Pitied but not entitled: Single mothers and the history of welfare, 1890-1935.* New York, NY: Free Press.

Grady, S. (2000). *Drama and diversity: A pluralistic perspective for educational drama.* Westport, CT: Heinemann.

Grayson, D. (1986). T*he equity principal: An inclusive approach to excellence.* Downey, CA: Los Angeles County Office of Education.

Grayson, D. A. (1985). *Infusing an equity agenda into schools districts.* Downey, CA: Los Angeles County Office of Education.

Gregory, A., Skiba, R. J., & Noguera, P. A. (2010). The achievement gap and the discipline gap: Two sides of the same coin? *Educational Researcher, 39*(1), 59–68.

Grossman, H. (1984). *Educating Hispanic children: Cultural implications for classroom instruction, classroom management, counseling, and assessment.* Springfield, IL: C. C. Thomas.

Guimond, S. (2000). Group socialization and prejudice: The social transmission of intergroup attitudes and beliefs. *European Journal of Social Psychology, 30*(3), 335–54.

Gutierrez, K. (2008). Developing a sociocritical literacy in the third space. *Reading Research Quarterly, 43*, 148–64.

Hancock, A. M. (2004). *The politics of disgust: The public identity of the welfare queen.* New York, NY: New York University Press.

Hatzenbuehler, M. L., McLaughlin, K. A., Keyes, K. M., & Hasin, D. S. (2010). The Impact of institutional discrimination on psychiatric disorders in lesbian, gay, and bisexual populations: A prospective study. *American Journal of Public Health, 100*(3), 452–59.

Henkel, K. E., Dovidio, J. F., & Gaertner, S. L. (2006). Institutional discrimination, individual racism, and Hurricane Katrina. *Analyses of Social Issues and Public Policy, 6(*1), 99–124.

Hill, J. D., & Flynn, K. M. (2006). *Classroom instruction that works with English language learners.* Alexandria, VA: Association for Supervision and Curriculum Development.

Iwamoto, D. (2003). Tupac Shakur: Understanding the identity formation of hyper-masculinity of a popular hip-hop artist. *The Black Scholar, 33*(2), 44–49.

Jenlink, P. M. (Ed.). (2009). *Equity issues for today's educational leaders: Meeting the challenge of creating equitable schools for all.* Lanham, MD: Rowman & Littlefield.

Kessler-Harris, A. (2003). *Pursuit of equity: Women, men, and the quest for economic citizenship in twentieth-century America.* Oxford, UK: Oxford University Press.

Ladson-Billings, G. (1995). Toward a theory of culturally relevant pedagogy. American *Educational Research Journal, 32*, 465–91.

Ladson-Billings, G. (2004). Landing on the wrong note: The price we paid for *Brown. Educational Researcher, 33*(7), 3–13.

Ladson-Billings, G. (2012). Through a glass darkly: The persistence of race in education research and scholarship. *Educational Researcher, 41*(4), 115–20.

Ladson-Billings, G., & Tate, E. (1995). Toward a critical race theory of education. *Teachers College Record, 97*(1), 47–67.

Lan Rong, X. (1996). Effects of race and gender on teachers' perceptions of the social behavior of elementary students. *Urban Education, 31*(3), 261–90.

Landsman, J. (2009). *A white teacher talks about race.* Lanham, MD: Rowman & Littlefield.

Laycock, D., & Picarello, Jr. A. (2008). *Same-sex marriage and religious liberty: Emerging conflicts.* Lanham, MD: Rowman & Littlefield.

Lee, C. D. (2003). Why we need to re-think race and ethnicity in educational research. *Educational Researcher*, *32*(5), 3–5.

Lemert, C., & Bhan, E. (1998). *The voice of Anna Julia Copper: Including a voice from the south and other important essays, papers, and letters* (Legacies of social thought series). Lenham, MD: Rowman & Littlefield.

Lensmire, T. J., & Snaza, N. (2010). What teacher education can learn from blackface minstrelsy. *Educational Researcher*, *39*(5), 413–22.

Lewis, C. W., Butler, B. R., Bonner, I. I., Fred, A., & Joubert, M. (2010). African American male discipline patterns and school district responses resulting impact on academic achievement: Implications for urban educators and policy makers. *Journal of African American Males in Education*, *1*(1), 7–25.

Lickel, B., Schmader, T., & Hamilton, D. L. (2003). A case of collective responsibility: Who else was to blame for the Columbine High School shootings? *Personality and Social Psychology Bulletin*, *29*(2), 194–204.

Lightfoot, S. L., & Carew, J. (1979). *Beyond bias: Perspectives on classrooms*. Cambridge, MA: Harvard University Press.

Livingston, J. N., & Nahimana, C. (2006). Problem child or problem context: An ecological approach to young black males. *Reclaiming Children and Youth*, *14*(4), 209.

Martin, J. L. (Ed.). (2015). *Racial battle fatigue: Insights from the front lines of social justice advocacy*. Santa Barbara, CA: Praeger.

Martin, J. L. (Ed.). (2011). *Women as leaders in education: Succeeding despite inequity, discrimination, and other challenges. Volume 1: Women as leaders in higher education*. Santa Barbara, CA: Praeger.

Martin, J. L. (Ed.). (2011). *Women as leaders in education: Succeeding despite inequity, discrimination, and other challenges. Volume 2: Women as leaders in classrooms and schools*. Santa Barbara, CA: Praeger.

Massaro, T. (2011). *Living justice: Catholic social teaching action*. Lanham, MD: Rowman & Littlefield.

McCarthy, J. D., & Hoge, D. R. (1987). The social construction of school punishment: Racial disadvantage out of universalistic process. *Social Forces*, *65*(4), 1101–20.

McCrudden, C. (1982). Institutional discrimination. *Oxford Journal of Legal Studies*, *2*(3), 303–67.

Milner, H. R. (2006). Preservice teachers' learning about cultural and racial diversity: Implications for urban education. *Urban Education*, *41*(4), 343–75.

Milner, H. R. (2008). Disrupting deficit notions of difference: Counter-narratives of teachers and community in urban education. *Teaching and Teacher Education*, *24*, 1573–98.

Milner, H. R. (Ed.) (2009). *Diversity and education: Teachers, teaching, and teacher education*. Springfield, IL: Charles C. Thomas Publisher.

Milner, H. R. (Ed.) (2010). *Culture, curriculum, and identity in education*. New York, NY: Palgrave Macmillan.

Milner, H. R. (2010). *Start where you are but don't stay there: Understanding diversity, opportunity gaps, and teaching in today's classrooms*. Cambridge, MA: Harvard Education Press.

Milner, H. R. (2012). Losing the color-blind mind in the urban classroom. *Urban Education*, *47*(5), 868–75.

Milner, H. R. (2015). *Racing to class: What schools should know and do to end poverty*. Cambridge, MA: Harvard Education Press.

Milner, H. R., & Lomotey, K. (Ed.) (2014). *Handbook of urban education*. New York, NY: Routledge Press.

Milner, H. R., & Ross, E. W. (Eds.) (2006). *Race, ethnicity, and education: The influences of racial and ethnic identity in education*. Westport, CT: Greenwood/Praeger.

Milner, H. R., Tenore, F. B., & Laughter, J. (2008). What can teacher education programs do to prepare teachers to teach high achieving culturally diverse males? *Gifted Child Today*, *31*(1), 18–23.

Milner, H. R., & Woolfolk Hoy, A. (2003). A case study of an African American teacher's self-efficacy, stereotype threat, and persistence. *Teaching and Teacher Education*, *19*, 263–76.

Moghadam, V. M. (2012). Globalization and social movements: Islamism, feminism, and the global justice movement (2nd ed.). Lanham, MD: Rowman & Littlefield.

Moll, L., & Gonzalez, N. (1994). Lessons from research with language minority children. *Journal of Reading Behavior, 26*(4), 23–41.

Monroe, C. R. (2005). Why are "bad boys" always black? Causes of disproportionality in school discipline and recommendations for change. *The Clearing House: A Journal of Educational Strategies, Issues and Ideas, 79*(1), 45–50.

Morris, J. E., & Monroe, C. R. (2009). Why study the U.S. south? The nexus of race and place in investigating black student achievement. *Educational Researcher, 38*(1), 21–36.

Morrison, A. M. (1993). *The new leaders: Guidelines on leadership diversity in America.* San Francisco, CA: Jossey-Bass.

Nadasen, P. (2005). *Welfare warriors: The welfare rights movement in the United States.* New York, NY: Routledge.

National Council of LaRaza. (1986). *The education of Hispanics: Status and implications.* Washington, DC: National Council of LaRaza.

Neelsen, J. P. (1975). Education and social mobility. *Comparative Education Review, 19*(1), 129–43.

Nieto, S. 4th. (2004). *Affirming diversity.* New York, NY: Longman.

Oaks, J. (1985). *Keeping track: How schools structure inequality.* New Haven, CT: Yale University Press.

Obiakor, F. E., & Algorzine, B. (2001). *It even happens in 'good' schools: Responding to cultural diversity in today's classrooms.* Thousand Oaks, CA: Corwin Press.

O'Connor, A. (2001). *Poverty knowledge: Social science, social policy, and the poor in twentieth-century U.S. history.* Princeton, NJ: Princeton University Press.

O'Connor, C., & Fernandez, S. D. (2006). Race, class, and disproportionality: Reevaluating the relationship between poverty and special education placement. *Educational Researcher, 35*(6), 6–11.

Okoye-Johnson, O. (2011). Does multicultural education improve students' racial attitudes? Implications for closing the achievement gap. *Journal of Black Studies, 42*(8), 1252–74.

Paris, D. (2012). Culturally sustaining pedagogy: A needed change in stance, terminology, and practice. *Educational Researcher, 41*(3), 93–97.

Penner, A. M., & Saperstein, A. (2013). Engendering racial perceptions: An intersectional analysis of how social status shapes race. *Gender & Society, 27*(3), 319–44.

Perry, B. L., & Morris, E. W. (2014). Suspending progress collateral consequences of exclusionary punishment in public schools. *American Sociological Review, 79*(6), 1067–87.

Pignatelli, F. & Pflaum, S. (1993). *Celebrating diverse voices: Progressive education and equity.* Newbury, CA: Corwin.

Pitre, A., Allen, T. G., & Pitre, E. (2015). *Multicultural education for educational leaders: Critical race theory and antiracist perspectives.* Lanham, MD: Rowman & Littlefield.

Purcell-Gates, V. (1995). *Other people's words: The cycle of low literacy.* Cambridge, MA: Harvard University Press.

Quadagno, J. (1994). *The color of welfare: How racism undermined the war on poverty.* New York, NY: Oxford University Press.

Reyhner, J. (1986). *Teaching the Indian child: A bilingual/multicultural approach.* Billing, MT: Eastern Montana College.

Rhoads, R. A. (1998). *Freedom's web: Student activism in an age of cultural diversity.* Baltimore, MD: Johns Hopkins.

Rios, F., & Rogers, C. A. (2011). *Understanding multicultural education: Equity for all students.* Lanham, MD: Rowman & Littlefield.

Ryan, J. (2006). *Inclusive leadership.* San Francisco, CA: Jossey-Bass.

Sadker, M., & Sadker D. (1990). *Sex equity handbook for schools.* New York: Longman.

Sampson, R. J., & Raudenbush, S. W. (2004). Seeing disorder: Neighborhood stigma and the social construction of "broken windows." *Social Psychology Quarterly, 67*(4), 319–42.

Scherff, L., & Spector, K. (Eds.). (2011). *Culturally relevant pedagogy: Clashes and confrontations.* Lanham, MD: Rowman & Littlefield.

Seller, M. S. (1988). *To seek America: A history of ethnic life in the United States.* Englewood, NJ: Jerome S. Ozer.

Servais, K. (2012). *The courage to grow: Leading with intentionality.* Lanham, MD: Rowman & Littlefield.

Sharma, A., Joyner, A. M., & Osment, A. (2014). Adverse impact of racial isolation on student performance: A study in North Carolina. *Education Policy Analysis Archives, 22*(14).

Sharp-Grier, Martina. (2015). "She was more intelligent than I thought she'd be!": Intersectionalities, stigma, and microaggressions in the academy. In J. L. Martin (Ed.), *Racial battle fatigue: insights from the front lines of social justice advocacy.* Westport, CT: Prager.

Sleeter, C. E. (2013). Becoming white: Reinterpreting a family story by putting race back into the picture. *Race Ethnicity and Education, 14*(4), 421–33.

Schlesinger, M., Dorwart, R., Hoover, C., & Epstein, S. (1997). The determinants of dumping: a national study of economically motivated transfers involving mental health care. *Health Services Research, 32*(5), 561.

Shipler, David. (2005). *The working poor: Invisible in America.* New York, NY: Vintage Books.

Skiba, R. J., Michael, R. S., Nardo, A. C., & Peterson, R. L. (2002). The color of discipline: Sources of racial and gender disproportionality in school punishment. *The Urban Review, 34*(4), 317–42.

Skiba, R., & Peterson, R. (1999). The dark side of zero tolerance: Can punishment lead to safe schools? *Phi Delta Kappan, 80*(5), 372–82.

Smith, W. A., Altbach, P. G., & Lomotey, K. (2002). *The racial crisis in American higher education: Continuing challenges for the twenty-first century* (Frontiers in Education). New York, NY: SUNY Press.

Smitherman, G. (2006). *Word from the mother: Language and African Americans.* New York, NY: Routledge.

Spencer, J. P. (2012). "Cultural deprivation" to cultural capital: The roots and continued relevance of compensatory education. *Teachers College Record, 114*(6), 1–5.

Spencer, M. B. (2008). Lessons learned and opportunities ignored since *Brown v. Board of Education*: Youth development and the myth of a colorblind society. *Educational Researcher, 37*(5), 253–66.

Spencer-Rodgers, J., & McGovern, T. (2002). Attitudes toward the culturally different: The role of intercultural communication barriers, affective responses, consensual stereotypes, and perceived threat. *International Journal of Intercultural Relations, 26*(6), 609–31.

Spring, J. (1985). *American education.* White Plains, NY: Longman.

Spring, J. (1989). *The sorting machine.* White Plains, NY: Longman.

Spring, J. (2004). *Deculturalization and the struggle for equality.* Boston, MA. McGraw Hill.

Spring, J. (2012). *Deculturalization and the struggle for equality: A brief history of the education of dominated cultures in the United States.* New York, NY: McGraw Hill.

Steele, C. M., & Aronson, J. (1995). Stereotype threat and the intellectual test performance of African Americans. *Journal of Personality and Social Psychology, 69*(5), 797–811.

Stephan, W. G., & Stephan, C. W. (2000). An integrated threat theory of prejudice. In S. Oskamp (Ed.) *Reducing prejudice and discrimination* (pp. 23–45). Mahwah, NJ: Lawrence Erlbaum and Associates.

Stevenson, B. (2014). *A just mercy: A story of justice and redemption.* New York, NY: Random House.

Straubhaar, R. (2015). The stark reality of the "White saviour" complex and the need for critical consciousness: A document analysis of the early journals of a Freirean educator. *Compare: A Journal of Comparative and International Education, 45*(3), 381–400.

Suad Nasir, N., & Saxe, G. B. (2003). Ethnic and academic identities: A cultural practice perspective on emerging tensions and their management in the lives of minority students. *Educational Researcher, 32*(5), 14–18.

Tatum, B. D. (1997). *Why are all the black kids sitting together in the cafeteria: And other conversations about race.* New York, NY: Basic Books.

Teidt, P. L., & Teidt, I. M. (2009). *Multicultural teaching: A handbook of activities, information, and resources.* New York, NY: Pearson.

Tocluk, S. (2010). *Witnessing whiteness: The need to talk about race and how to do it.* Lanham, MD: Rowman and Littlefield.

Thompson, C. (1985). *As boys become men: Learning new male roles.* Cambridge, MA: Resources for Change.

Wallace, T. L., & Chhuon, V. (2014). Proximal processes in urban classrooms: Engagement and disaffection in urban youth of color. *American Educational Research Journal, 51*(5), 937–73.

Ward, J., & Anthony, P. (1992). *Who pays for student diversity? Population changes and educational policy.* Newbury Park, CA: Corwin.

Weinberg, M. (1986). *Because they were Jews: A history of anti-Semitism.* Westport, CT: Greenwood Press.

Wells, A. S. (1989). Hispanic education in America: Separate and unequal. *New York. ERIC Clearinghouse on Urban Education 59*, Teachers College, Columbia University.

Wiggins, G. (1991). Standards not standardization: Evoking quality student work. *Educational Leadership, 48*(5), 18–20.

Wildhagen, T. (2012). How teachers and schools contribute to racial differences in the realization of academic potential. *Teachers College Record, 114*(7), 1–27.

Zion, S. D., & Blanchett, W. (2011). (Re)conceptualizing inclusion: Can critical race theory and interest convergence be utilized to achieve inclusion and equity for African American students? *Teachers College Record, 113*(10), 22186–205.

Index

www.ingramcontent.com/pod-product-compliance
Lightning Source LLC
Chambersburg PA
CBHW021819270326
41932CB00007B/261